BLESS THIS HOME AND BASKET
PAGES 62, 63

NOAH'S ARK
PAGES 34, 35

WATCHES
PAGE 71

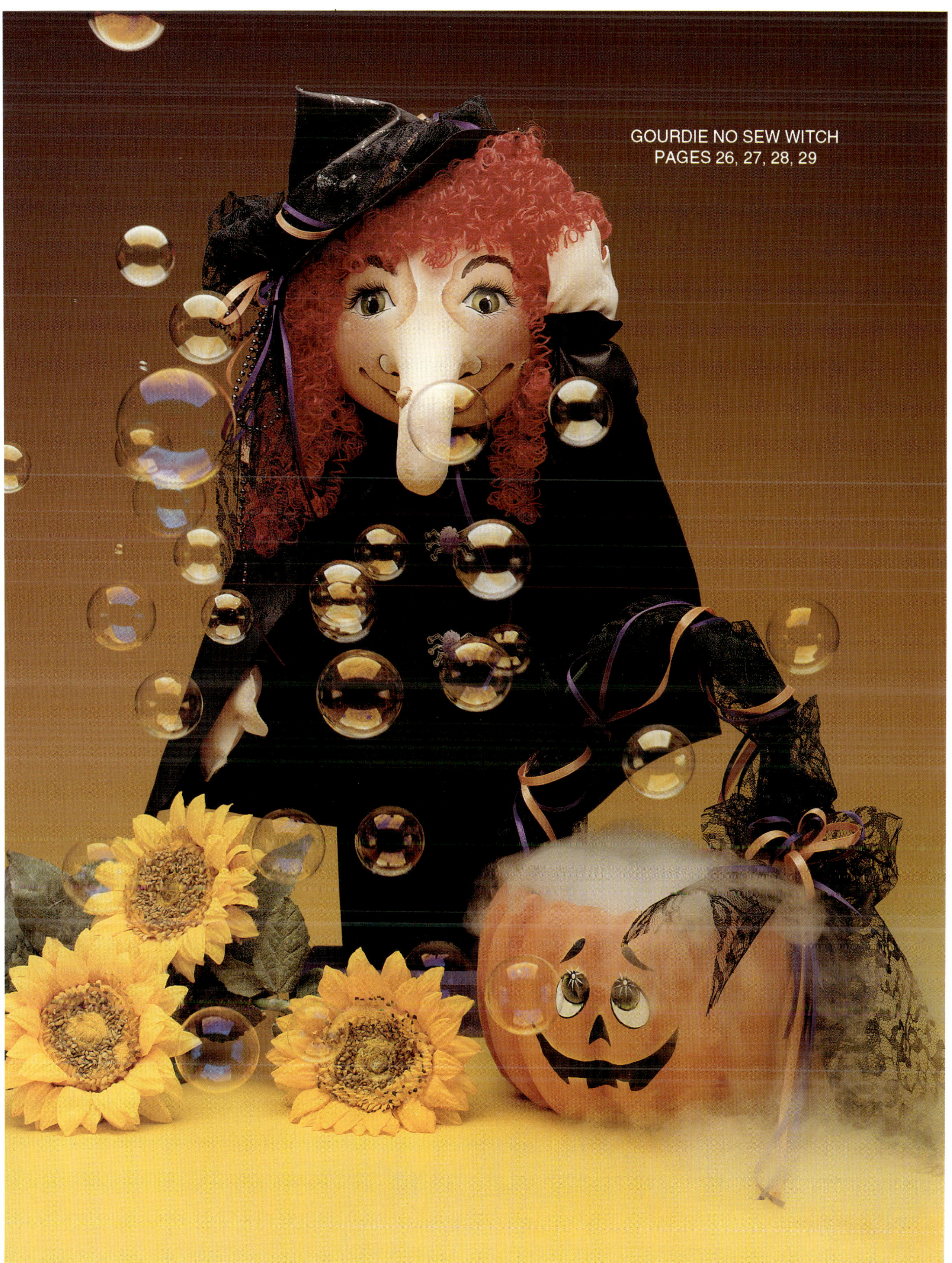
GOURDIE NO SEW WITCH
PAGES 26, 27, 28, 29

FLOWER CART AND GOURD
PAGES, 38, 48, 49

13435 NE Whitaker Way, Portland, Oregon 97230
Phone (503) 254-9100

DEDICATION

What is a home without a Mother-in law? What is a Mother-in-law without horror stories? A Mother-in-law at my house is some poor lady who gets stuck base painting mountains of wood, and maybe gets a Sunday dinner out of the deal. She is truly the only one who can raise cane with the man I'm married to and gets away with it. She has also gracefully consented to be a Great Grandmother, of course only so that I can be a Grandmother. (There's another plus for being Granny). Thank God for one of the many blessings he has bestowed on me in the form of the dreaded Mother-in-law. What a sweetheart Dorris Thornton is. A special thanks for all of her help.

Believe me my life is truly not all a bed of roses. But when you feel down you can always look around and see somebody further down. Try counting your blessings on a really bad day and see how well it works.

Color Comparison Chart

All symbols key on the DecoArt color:
A (+) by another company's color means that the color family is the same, but the other company's color is darker than DecoArt.
A (-) by another company's color means that the color family is the same, but the other company's color is lighter than DecoArt.
An (*) by the DecoArt color means that no other company has a reasonably comparative color to our knowledge.

These comparisons were compared dry to dry. As some companies vary their colors slightly in different batches, please be aware that the colors will be close but seldom exact. This color comparison chart is as close as representative samples as possible, however, DecoArt does not guarantee the identical color matches of competitive colors. This is only a general guide for companrison.

COLORS	DECOART AMERICANA (DA)	DELTA CERAMCOAT	PLAID FOLKART	ILLINOIS BRONZE ACCENT & COUNTRY COLORS
WHITES	DA1 Snow White		901 Wicker White	2476 Real White
	DA2 White Wash	E White		2454 White Wash
	DA3 Buttermilk	2001 Antique White	903 Tapioca	2428 Off White
	DA4 Sand	2036 Ivory	902 Taffy	2311 Adobe Wash
	DA77 Desert Sand		703 Vanilla Cream	
	DA89 Cool Neutral	2402 Sandstone	857 Porcelain White	
	DA90 Warm Neutral		704 Milkshake	
YELLOWS	(*)DA5 Taffy Cream			
	DA6 Pineapple	2005 Pale Yellow		2306 Cactus Flower
	(*)DA7 Moon Yellow			
	DA8 Yellow Ochre	(-)2092 Old Parchment	737 Butter Crunch	
	DA9 Antique Gold	2003 Oaktone		
	DA10 Cadmium Yellow	D Yellow		736 School Bus Yellow
	DA11 Lemon Yellow	2064 Sunbright Yellow	(+)918 Sunny Yellow	2410 Mellow Yellow
		(+)2027 Bright Yellow	735 Lemon Custard	
		2004 Luscious Lemon		
		(-)2101 Pineapple		
	(*)DA93 Raw Sienna			
ORANGES	DA12 Tangerine	2028 Native Flesh		
		2042 Pumpkin		
	DA13 Pumpkin	(+)2026 Orange		2473 True Orange
		(+)2043 Tangerine		
	DA14 Cadmium Orange		920 Autumn Leaves	2573 Floral Orange
	(*)DA15 Cadmium Red			
	DA16 Burnt Orange	2097 Georgia Clay		
	DA17 Georgia Clay	2030 Burnt Sienna		
		2020 Red Iron Oxide		
	DA102 Medium Flesh	2126 Medium Flesh		2420 Peaches 'n Cream

COLORS	DECOART AMERICANA (DA)	DELTA CERAMCOAT	PLAID FOLKART	ILLINOIS BRONZE ACCENT & COUNTRY COLORS
REDS	DA18 Country Red	2098 Tomato Spice	931 Red Clay	2302 Pueblo Red
	DA19 Berry Red	2107 Tompt Red	932 Calico Red	2470 Pure Red
				2449 Jo Sonja Red
	DA20 Calico Red	C Bright Red		2579 Razzle Red
	DA21 Crimson Tide	2075 Maroon	758 Cherry Royale	2332 Bordeauz
			935 Raspberry Wine	2421 Holiday Red
	DA22 Burgundy Wine	2130 Sweetheart Blush	(-)957 Burgundy	
		2125 Pthalo Crimson		
	DA79 Brandy Wine	2123 Burgundy Rose	847 Apple Spice	
	DA80 Russet	2407 Candy Bar	757 Brownie	
	DA96 Red Iron Oxide	2020 Red Iron Oxide	914 Rusty Nail	2424 Barn Red
	DA97 Rookwood Red	2446 Sonoma	756 Chocolate Cherry	2425 Fingerberry Red
	(*)DA104 Napthol Red	2408 Napthol Crimson		
	DA112 Cranberry Wine		935 Raspberry Wine	
PINKS MAUVES PURPLES	DA23 Peaches & Cream	(-)2433 Island Coral	(+)911 Apricot Cream	2319 L 'Orangerie
	DA24 Flesh	(-)2033 Dresden Flesh		
	DA25 Dusty Rose	(-)2018 Indiana Rose	752 Berries 'N Cream	2452 Victorian Mauve
		2432 Normandy Rose	(-)929 Cotton Candy	
	DA26 Mauve	2132 Bouquet	753 Rose Chiffon	2450 Roseberry
	DA27 Gooseberry	2129 Gypsy Rose	(-)912 Promenade	
	DA28 Raspberry	2405 Dusty Mauve		
	(*)DA29 Boysenberry			
	DA30 Spice Pink		955 Sweetheart Pink	
	(*)DA31 Baby Pink			
	(*)DA32 Lilac			
	DA33 Orchid	(+)2403 Lilac Dust		
		2060 Lilac		
	DA34 Lavender		(-)933 Heather	2475 True Purple
				2304 Purple Canyon
	DA101 Dioxazine Purple	2015 Purple		
	DA103 Coral Rose	2045 Fiesta Pink		
	DA110 Blush			

COLORS	DECOART AMERICANA (DA)	DELTA CERAMCOAT	PLAID FOLKART	ILLINOIS BRONZE ACCENT & COUNTRY COLORS
BLUES	DA35 Navy Blue	2114 Midnight	906 Indigo	2446 Indigo Blue
	DA36 True Blue	(-)2124 Manganese Blue		2472 Pure Blue
		2089 Navy Blue		2412 Ultra Marine Blue
		2051 Copen Blue		
		B Phalo Blue		
	DA37 Blueberry	2131 Nightfal		
	(*)DA38 Wedgewood Blue			
	DA39 Victorian Blue			(-)2563 Larkspur Blue
	DA40 Williamsburg Blue	(-)2069 Wedgewood Blue		2440 Stoneware Blue
		2133 Cape Cod		
	(*)DA41 Country Blue			
	DA42 Baby Blue	2037 Blue Heaven		
	(*)DA43 Salem Blue			
	DA44 Desert Turquoise	2058 Colonial Blue		
	DA81 Colonial Green			2451 Village Green
	DA85 Midnight Blue	2413 Prusian Blue	964 Midnight	2439 Liberty Blue
	DA86 Uniform Blue	2114 Midnight	(+)975 Slate Blue	2441 Soldier Blue
	DA87 Indian Turquoise		722 Baby Blue	(+)2307 Nevada Turquoise
	DA98 French Blue	2133 Cape Cod		2440 Stoneware Blue
	(*)DA99 Sapphire			
	DA100 Ultra Deep Blue	2038 Ultra Marine Blue		
	DA105 Blue Grey Mist		758 Blue Grey Dust	
	DA115 Blue Haze			2310 Prairie Green
GREENS	DA45 Mint Julep		(+)915 Robin's Egg	
	(*)DA46 Sea Aqua			
	DA47 Bluegrass Green	2115 Blue Spruce		
	DA48 Holly Green	2068 Christmas Green		2577 Holiday Green
	DA49 Dark Pine	2100 Woodland Night	725 Tartar Green	2310 Prairie Green
	(*)DA50 Forest Green			
	DA51 Leaf Green	2420 Dark Jungle	327 Old Ivy	2442 Green Olive
			926 Shamrock	
	DA52 Avacado	2420 Dark Jungle	952 Fipe Avocado	2320 Chateau Moss
			(-)928 Patchwork Green	
			(-)923 Clover	
GREENS	DA53 Mistletoe	2011 Chrome Greebn Lt		
	(*)DA54 Bright Green			
	DA55 Kelly Green	2008 Green Isle		
	DA56 Olive Green	2067 Leaf Green	954 Fresh Foliage	
	DA57 Jade Green	(+)2422 Leprechaun	922 Bayberry	
		2070 Wedgewood Green		
	DA82 Evergreen	2010 Forest Green	924 Thicket	2445 Pine Needle Green
	DA83 Black Forest	2096 Dark Forest	727 Parrot Green	2444 Deep Forest Green
	DA84 Midnight Green	2116 Black Green	925 Wrought Iron	
	DA106 Lt. Avocado		728 Green Olive	2438 Chesapeake Blue
	(*)DA108 Viridian Green	A Pthalo Green		
	DA113 Plantation Pine		730 Southern Pine	
	DA116 Deep Teal			2438 Chesapeake Blue

COLORS	DECOART AMERICANA (DA)	DELTA CERAMCOAT	PLAID FOLKART	ILLINOIS BRONZE ACCENT & COUNTRY COLORS
BROWNS	DA58 Antique White	(-)2402 Sandstone	(+)939 Butter Pecan	2453 Wicker
	DA59 Toffee	2085 AC Flesh		
	DA60 Mocha	(-)2019 Fleshtone		
	DA61 Sable Brown	2425 Territorial Beige		
	DA62 Terra Cotta	(+)2055 Autumn Brown		
		2086 Toffee		
	DA63 Burnt Sienna	2023 Brown Iron Oxide	945 Maple Syrup	2435 Burnt Sienna
			943 Molasses	
	DA64 Burnt Umber	2053 Dark Brown	940 Coffee Bean	2408 Sweet Chocolate
	DA65 Dark Chocolate	2024 Walnut	950 Chocolate Fudge	2437 Burnt Umber
		2025 Burnt Umber		
	DA78 Flesh Tone	2125 Medium Flesh	949 Skintone	
	DA91 Cashmere Beige	2033 Dresden Flesh	705 Almond Parfait	
	DA92 Mink Tan	2424 Bambi	706 Chocolait Parfait	
	DA94 Mississippi Mud	2109 Brown Velvet		2436 Raw Sienna
	DA109 Taupe			
	DA114 Lt. Cinnamon			
BLACKS GREYS	DA67 Ebony Black	F Black	938 Licorice	2477 Real Black
	(*)DA88 Charcoal Grey			
	(*)DA68 Slate Grey			
	DA69 Dove Grey	(+)2426 Cadet Grey		
	(*)DA95 Neutral Grey	2090 Hippo Grey		
	DA111 Grey Sky			
METALLICS	DA70 Shimmering Silver		No Comparable Product	
	DA71 Glorious Gold		No Comparable Product	
	DA72 Venetian Gold		No Comparable Product	
	DA73 Bronze		No Comparable Product	
	DA74 Royal Ruby		No Comparable Product	
	DA75 Ice Blue		No Comparable Product	
	DA76 Crystal Green		No Comparable Product	
SPECIALIZED PRODUCTS	DAS1 Brush 'n Blend (Extender)	8001 Acry Blend	947 Extender	
	DAS10 Fabric Painting Medium	300 Textile Medium	794 Fabric Medium	
	DAS11 Control Medium (Thickner)		948 Thickner	

DecoArt™

Box 360, Stanford, KY 40484 (606)365-3193 Toll-Free (800)367-3047 Fax (606)365-9739

How To's and What Are's

Fl. = Floating:

Floating is extremely important so practice it. It is used to do almost all of the shading and highlighting in this book. Unless otherwise stated for instance, highlight with White tole stroke. First load your brush in water, pat on a paper towel until you cannot see the water seeping out of the brush. Side load your brush and blend on the palette before going to your piece. The desired result is heavy paint on the side that you loaded fading to nothing on the opposite corner. If you can see paint coming off from both sides of the brush when you begin to work it is improperly loaded.

Rinse and start again.

Basing in:

Is simply filling in an entire area in one color. But it is very important, it is the basis for all of the following detail work. When basing in an area start in the center of the object and push the paint to the edge. By using this method you will not leave little ridges between your color changes which makes your floating and liner work much simpler to do. Even smooth coverage is what you are after.

Wet in Wet:

Apply a basecoat, while this is still wet work in your other colors. This method gives a soft blend on the edges but leaves true color in the center. Works well with stippling.

Stippling:

Is used a lot in fur, shrubs, flowers and etc. Load one of those good old ruined brushes you were going to throw out, use a straight up and down patting motion. Very effective when used with more then one color.

Wash:

Is paint thinned with water, it is generally a full loaded brush to cover an entire area. When working a large area it helps to dampen the wood first so you won't leave brush strokes. It leaves a very transparent look, is very nice on new wood because you can still see the grain.

Spattering:

Use an old tooth brush. Dip in paint thinned with water, run your finger nail or similar sharp object through the bristles. The more water that you add the larger your spatters will be.

Double load:

Dip one corner of the brush in one color and the other corner in a different color. Work back and forth on your palette to blend the two colors in the center. Do not over blend you still want pure color from each corner. Example load Dk. Forest on one corner and Apple Green on the opposite. Blend on the palette and presto leaves in one stroke.

Miskit:

Is a liquid latex product that when applied protects a painted area from the next coat of paint. It works the same as masking off the edge with tape. But is very handy because you can do small jagged areas that you can't do with tape. Always be sure to load your brush in a liquid detergent do not wash this out of your brush. This protects the bristles from the miskit and enables cleaning the brush when you are through. Paint miskit on very carefully do not slop it on, every place you miss a spot or leave a jagged edge the paint will adhere to. When miskit is throughly dry you may, paint, sponge or stain over it with complete protection to the paint underneath. Allow your paint to dry and peel off the miskit.

Synthetic Bristles:

Are man made fibers as opposed to true hair. They are generally a little less expensive and last a little longer in this type of work.

Stylus:

Is used for tracing designs and also to make nice dots. The advantage of a stylus in tracing your patterns is that it does not mark on your pattern. The disadvantage is (if you are a beginner) it does not leave lines, so be careful not to miss part of the tracing.

Antiquing:

Seal your piece with either 2 to 3 coats of good quality varnish or Tuffilm. When using Joyce Howard's Mudd, apply with a sponge brush. Begin by wiping off the excess with a lint free rag, then with a mop or a good white China bristle brush 2" or more (from local hardware store). Begin feathering the paint, drawing it towards the center and up and down. The end results should be a nice soft look with no brush strokes showing. After you have gotten it this far, highlight with a soft lint free rag, or if in a small area, a Q-tip. If you still want more highlight, let cure and hit very carefully with the finest steel wool that there is. When using oil paints, I prefer a mix of equal parts oil paint, thinner and Winsor Newton's Liquin. This makes a very nice creamy consistency that is easy to work with. Then use the same steps as for Mudd. Antiquing is a personal preference thing, it may be left on heavy or taken off almost completely.

PREPARING SURFACES

New Wood:

1. Sand burrs and fill in all holes, cracks and etc.

2. Use a tack cloth in between each step in preparation to pick up the dust.

3. Seal the piece according to the directions on the product you are using.

4. Sand the piece completely but be careful not to oversand. Acrylics need a tooth to hold on to. It should not feel like glass.

5. If you are staining do not seal the piece before hand. Sand lightly with #600.

6. If it is a painted background it may be sanded between coats with #600 for brush strokes that show.

7. Be sure to keep that tack cloth handy.

New and Old Metal or Tin:

New Metal or Tin:

1. Wipe the entire piece with white vinegar and water.

2. Apply auto body primer with a rust inhibitor. It doesn't come in many colors, but I try to choose one close to what I'm painting. Example: paint Burgundy Rose, primer Medium Brown.

Old Metal or Tin:

1. Very carefully remove all rust, dirt, paint, and etc. For those really tough cases, naval jelly from your local hardware store works well on old rust. When you have everything removed, follow the same steps as for new tin.

Fabric:

1. Always be sure and wash whatever fabric you are working on. This removes the sizing and also preshrinks before painting. Be very careful working with old articles of clothing. They build up fabric softener and soaps which repel the dyes. Old articles may be washed in a solution of vinegar and water. This helps, but is not guaranteed.

2. Never use fabric softeners. They are oily and repel the dyes.

3. Always use a fabric medium.

4. I always heat set with an iron. After all of that work, why take the chance on It fading when it only takes a few minutes to heat set.

SUPPLIES

All acrylic and fabric paints by DecoArt:

Acrylics:

Antique Gold
Black
Black Forest Green
Brandywine
Buttermilk
Burnt Umber
Burnt Sienna
Cadmium Orange
Calico Red
Colonial Green
Country Blue
Country Red
Cool Neutral
Peaches n Cream
Dioxazine Purple
Russet
Dusty Rose
Forest Green
French Blue Grey
Gooseberry
Grey Sky
Indian Turquoise
Jade Green
Lemon Yellow
Light Cinnamon
Mauve
Mink Tan
Mocha
Moon Yellow
Crimson Tide
Raw Sienna
Dark Pine
Terra Cotta
Toffee
True Blue
Sapphire Blue
Salem Blue
Sand
Skin Tone
Slate Grey
Uniform Blue
Wedgewood Blue
White
Williamsburg Blue
Cranberry Wine
Plantation Pine
Deep Teal
Rookwood Red

So Soft Fabric Paints:

Black
Burgundy Wine
Dark Chocolate
Grey Sky
Peaches n Cream
Flesh Tan
White
Williamsburg Blue
Golden Yellow

Heavy Metals: Glimmer

Shimmering Pearls: Christmas Green, Christmas Red, Golden Yellow, Ultra Blue

Dazzling Metallics:

Black Pearl
Glorious Gold
Green Pearl
Shimmering Silver
Teal Pearl
White Pearl
Ice Blue
Venetian Gold

BRUSHES

Stan Brown's brushes are new to the market by just a few weeks and I'm really pleased with the way they work.

Shader Series #910 Sizes 6, 8, 10, 12
Filbert Series # 912 Sizes 4 and 8
Grainier Series #919 Sizes 1/4 and 1/2
Script Series #914 Size 0
Liner Series #913 Size 1

SOURCES

Stan Brown Arts and Crafts
12435 N. E. Whitaker Way
Portland, Oregon 97230

The Lace Place
103 Church Road
Kelso, Wa. 98626

Todd Hupp
P. O. Box 1446
Clackamas, Or. 97015

Pottery: Rod Bennett, Wagon Wheel Pottery
P. O. Box 782
Crane, Oregon 97732

Plum Fun for small accent pieces:
5427 S. E. 72nd Avenue
Portland, Oregon 97206

BELLA COW

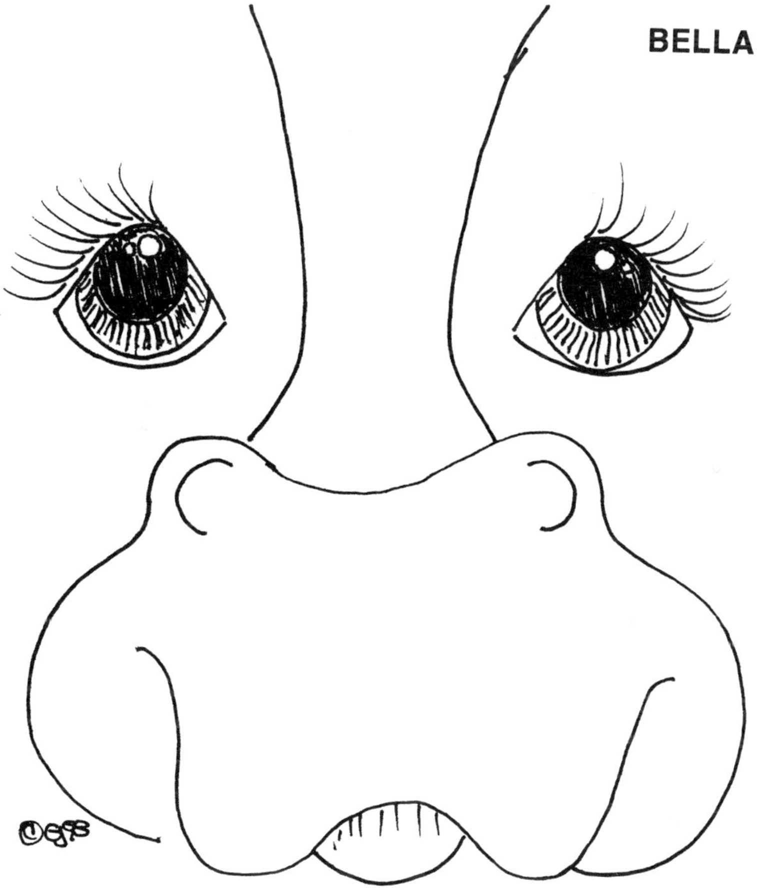

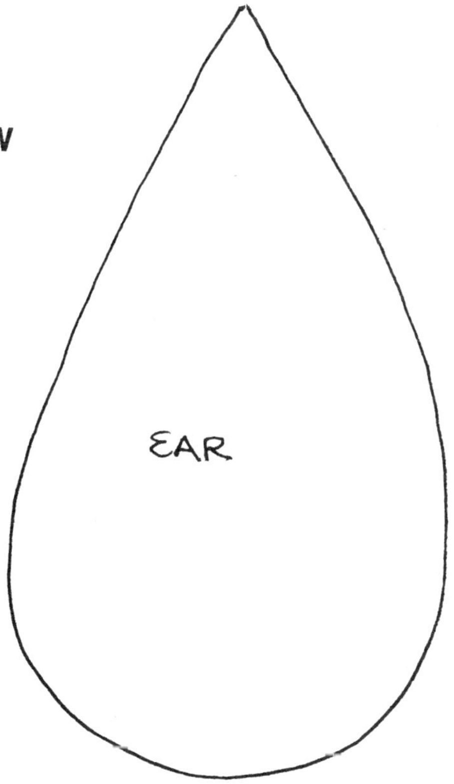

EAR

CUT 2 BLACK FELT
2 PINK FELT
WONDER UNDER
1 BLACK & 1 PINK
TOGETHER

PALETTE-Deco Art Americana
Black
Slate Grey
Light Cinnamon
Williamsburg Blue
Rookwood Red
Gooseberry
White
Mocha
Brandywine
True Blue
Mauve

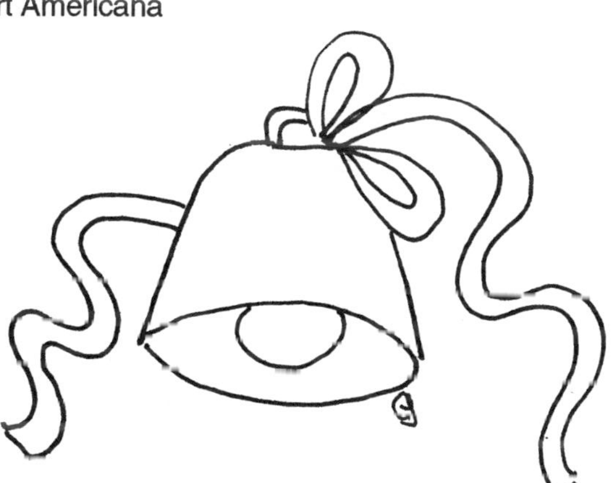

Miscellaneous Supplies
8" White Crochet Hat
2' of gathered 1-1/2" white lace
1-1/2' of gathered 1/2" white lace for apron
2 Yds. of paid 1" ribbon
2' of blue 1/4" ribbon
1 large silk flower
Stardust gyp
Wood excelsior for hair
4 Hearts 1/2"
1 Heart 1"
6" x 6" Square of Black and Pink Felt

1. Base her dress in a mix of 1/2 Mauve and 1/4 Brandywine. Do the stripes with a mix of White plus a touch of Williamsburg Blue. Float all of the shadows with Rookwood Red. Float the highlights with White plus a touch of the base mix.
2. Base the apron in White plus a touch of Williamsburg Blue. Float the shadows with Williamsburg Blue. Float the highlights with White. Do the tole strokes and the stitches in Williamsburg Blue plus a touch of Black.
3. Base the White areas on the cow in White plus a touch of Slate Grey. Float the shadows and base the hooves in Slate Grey. Float the shadows on the hooves and do all of the spots on the cow in Black. Float the highlights on the black areas and around the eyes with Slate Grey. Float the highlight on the hooves with White.
4. Base the muzzle in Mocha. Float the shadows with Light Cinnamon. Float the highlights with White plus a touch of Mocha. Pink up these areas with a light wash of Gooseberry.
5. Base her eyes in White. Do the iris in Williamsburg Blue. Float the bottom half of the iris in True Blue. Do the pupils and the lashes in Black, highlight with White.

Get out the glue gun and go wild with her hat. I'm into funky hats.

POT BELLY # 201
AVAILABLE: STAN BROWN'S

BELLA COW

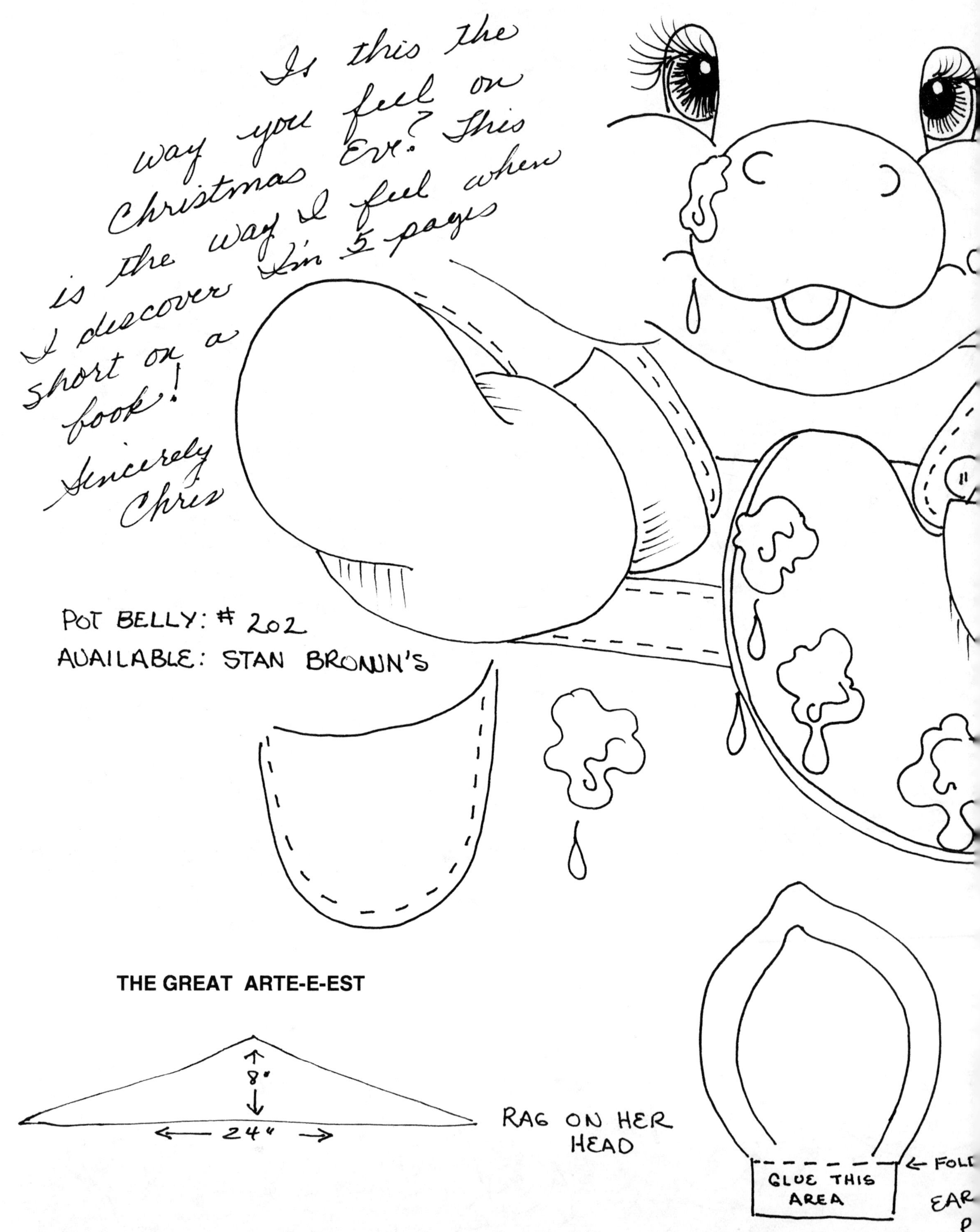

THE GREAT ARTE-E-EST

THE GREAT ARTE-E-ST

PALETTE-Deco Art Americana

Black
Moon Yellow
Slate Grey
Light Cinnamon
Mocha
Plantation Pine
Gooseberry
White
Buttermilk
Country Red
Uniform Blue

Miscellaneous Supplies:

One stripe of fabric 24" x 8"
One old brush
One silk flower
One sheet of watercolor paper

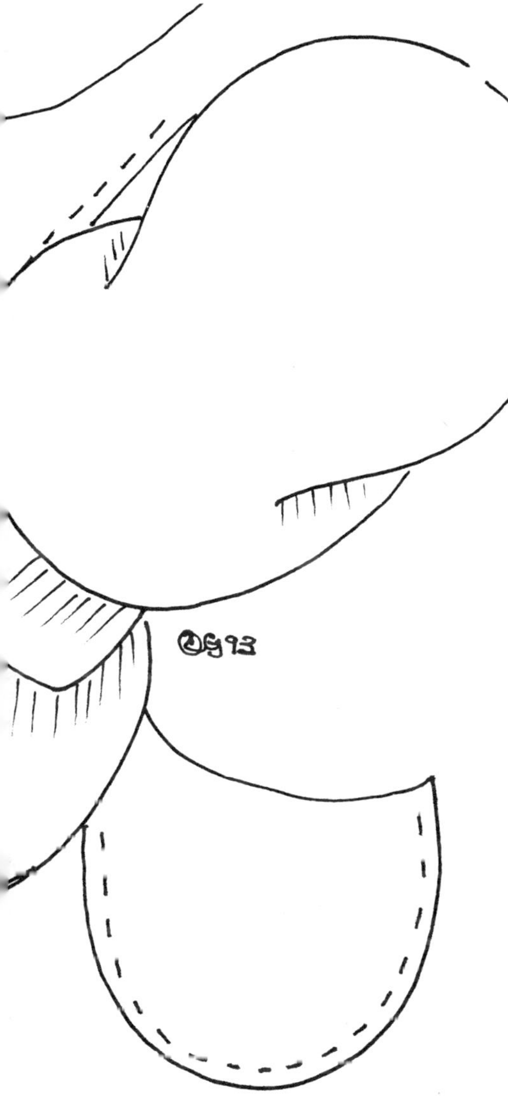

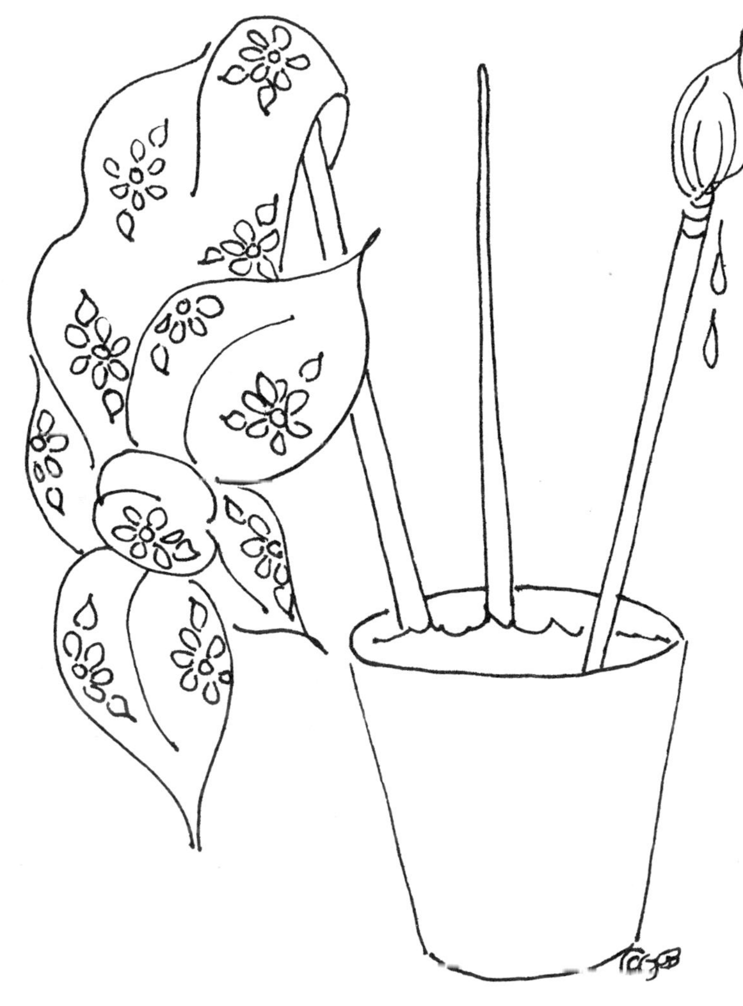

1. Base the pig and the ears on the watercolor paper in Mocha. Pink up all of these areas with a light wash of Gooseberry. Float the shadows with Light Cinnamon. Float the highlights with White plus a touch of Gooseberry.
2. Base the overalls in Uniform Blue. Float the shadows with Uniform Blue plus a touch of Black. Float the highlights with White plus a touch of Uniform Blue. Do all of the stitching in Mocha.
3. Base the palette and the eyes in White plus Buttermilk. Float the shadows on the palette in Light Cinnamon. Float the iris in the eyes and all of the green splotches of paint with Plantation Pine. Float the yellow splotches of paint and do the button on her pants in Moon Yellow. Float the red splotches of painting Country Red.
4. Base the hooves in Slate Grey. Float the shadows with Black and the highlights with White.
5. Do the pupils, lashes and line the whole piece in Black.

Poke a small hole in the pot belly to stick in the brush and another to stick in the silk flower.

HOG HEAVE
BOARD, FRAME, AND APPLES 3/4" pine
1 LEG 1/2" PINE
1 FOOT 1/4" BIRCH
WOOD AVAILABLE:
THE LACE PLACE

HOG HEAVEN

PALETTE-Deco Americana
Black
Moon Yellow
Calico Red
Sand
Gooseberry
White

Mocha
Buttermilk
Rookwood Red
French Blue Grey
Uniform Blue

Burnt Umber
Raw Sienna
Country Red
Slate Grey
Light Cinnamon

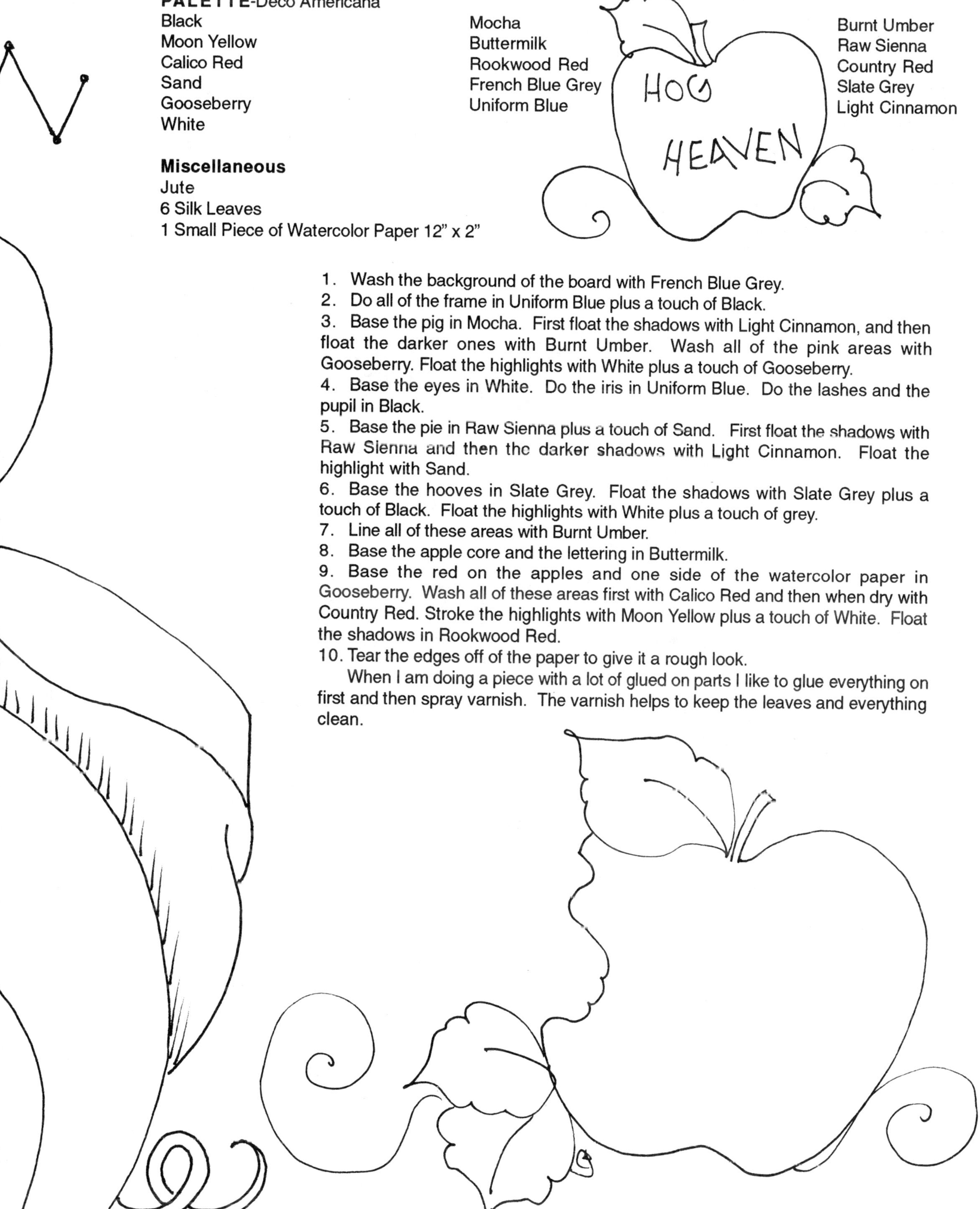

Miscellaneous
Jute
6 Silk Leaves
1 Small Piece of Watercolor Paper 12" x 2"

1. Wash the background of the board with French Blue Grey.
2. Do all of the frame in Uniform Blue plus a touch of Black.
3. Base the pig in Mocha. First float the shadows with Light Cinnamon, and then float the darker ones with Burnt Umber. Wash all of the pink areas with Gooseberry. Float the highlights with White plus a touch of Gooseberry.
4. Base the eyes in White. Do the iris in Uniform Blue. Do the lashes and the pupil in Black.
5. Base the pie in Raw Sienna plus a touch of Sand. First float the shadows with Raw Sienna and then the darker shadows with Light Cinnamon. Float the highlight with Sand.
6. Base the hooves in Slate Grey. Float the shadows with Slate Grey plus a touch of Black. Float the highlights with White plus a touch of grey.
7. Line all of these areas with Burnt Umber.
8. Base the apple core and the lettering in Buttermilk.
9. Base the red on the apples and one side of the watercolor paper in Gooseberry. Wash all of these areas first with Calico Red and then when dry with Country Red. Stroke the highlights with Moon Yellow plus a touch of White. Float the shadows in Rookwood Red.
10. Tear the edges off of the paper to give it a rough look.

When I am doing a piece with a lot of glued on parts I like to glue everything on first and then spray varnish. The varnish helps to keep the leaves and everything clean.

LITTLE CHILD ROBE RACK

PALETTE-Deco Americana

Baby Blue
Raspberry
Dark Chocolate
Teal Green
Light Cinnamon
White
Midnite Blue
Colonial Green
Sand
Blush
Uniform Blue
Black
Raw Sienna
Desert Sand
Terra Cotta
Mauve

Background

Base the background in Uniform Blue. On the last coat of Uniform Blue while it is still wet streak with Midnite Blue. Do the pegs and the banding in Midnite Blue.

CHILD TONIGHT

LITTLE CHILD ROBE RACK

Blanket

Base the blanket in Colonial Green. Alternate the stripes on the blanket in Raspberry and Colonial Green plus White. Float the shadows with Teal Green. Go back and float the darker shadows with Midnite Blue. Float the highlights with the light stripe mix. Float the lace on the edge of the blanket with Sand.

Bear

1. Base the sleeve in Mauve. Float the shadows with Raspberry and float the highlights and the lace with White.
2. Base the bear in 2:Raw Sienna and 1:Desert Sand. Float all of the shadows with Light Cinnamon. Stipple the highlights with Sand. Use Sand to stipple in the muzzle and then stipple the highlight on this with White.
3. Float the inside of the ears and the muzzle with Blush.

Bunny

1. Base the little bit of sleeve in Colonial Green. Float the shadows with Teal Green.
2. Base the bunny in Desert Sand. Float the shadows with a mix of 1/2 Desert Sand and 1/2 Light Cinnamon. Stipple all of the highlights with White.
3. Base the nose and float all of the pink areas on the bunny with Sand plus a touch of Blush.
4. Do all of the stitching on the bunny in Light Cinnamon.

Raccoon

1. Base the sleeve in Desert Sand, stripe with Uniform Blue. Float the shadows with Light Cinnamon and the highlights with White.
2. Base in Dark Chocolate plus a touch of Sand. Float the shadows in Dark Chocolate plus a touch of Black. Stipple the area around the eyes with Black. Stipple the highlights and the muzzle area with Sand plus a touch of Dark Chocolate.
3. Float the highlights on the eyes and do the lashes with Grey Sky.
4. Float the muzzle and the inside of the ears with Blush.

Tiger Cub

1. Base the sleeve in Baby Blue and stripe with Blush. Float the shadows with Uniform Blue and the highlight with White.
2. Base the tiger in Terra Cotta. Float all of the shadows in Dark Chocolate. Do the stripes in Black. Stipple all of the highlights with Desert Sand.
3. Float the inside of the ears and float the muzzle with Blush.

Do all of the noses, mouths and stitches on all of the animals except the bunny in Black. Highlight all facial features with White.

Lettering

Mix 1/2 Colonial Green and 1/2 Baby Blue and tole stroke in the lettering. Line on the left side with White.

Stars

Float first a circle of 1/2 Sand and 1/2 White. Streak the line and do the dots in the center of the star with the same mix. The dots are done in Sand, Baby Blue and Mauve plus a touch of White.

SUNNY AND WARM

PALETTE-Deco Americana So Soft Fabric Dyes

Antique Gold	Cranberry Wine	Avocado
Dark Chocolate	Black	Flesh Tan
Cadmium Yellow	Grey Sky	Calico Red
Victorian Blue	Christmas Green	White
Raspberry Pink		

1. With a ruler mark all of the check in 1/2"squares. Wash the blue squares with Victorian Blue.
2. Wash tho cow in White. Base all of the spots in Black. Float all of the shadows on the white areas and tho highlights on the black areas with Grey Sky plus a touch of Black.
3. Wash the pig, and calves nose and inside of the ears with Flesh Tan. Float the shadows on all of these areas with Dark Chocolate. Pink up all of these areas with Calico Red. Highlight all of the flesh areas with White plus a touch of Flesh Tan.
4. Wash all of the hooves in Grey Sky and float shadows with Black.
5. Wash the sun in Cadmium Yellow. Float the shadows with Antique Gold. Float the cheeks with Calico Red. Stipple the hair on the calf with these colors.
6. Wash all of the flowers and the bow with Raspberry Pink. Pat in the centers of the flowers and float the shadows on the bow with Cranberry Wine. Highlight the bow and do the petals on the flowers with White.
7. Wash all of the green areas around the flowers with Avocado. Go back in and wash the darker areas around the flowers with Christmas Green plus a touch of Dark Chocolate. With a #4 filbert do the dark green leaves with this mix. Do the small blue shadow leaves with Victorian Blue.
8. Do all of the lettering in Victorian Blue plus a touch of Black.
9. Do all of the outlines and divide squares with Black.

SUNNY AND WARM

GOURDIE NO SEW WITCH

Don't let this little witch fool you. She's quite simple and involves only 3 hand gathered seams so you don't have to be a seamstress. Everything is either hot glued or done with Wonder Under. But of course if you like to sew go for it.

PALETTE-Deco Americana

Berry Red
Grey Sky
Burnt Umber
Light Cinnamon
Coral Rose
White
Gooseberry
Black Forest Green
Lemon Yellow
Country Red
Mistletoe
Heavy Metal Silver
Black
Lavender
Cadmium Orange
Mocha
Dioxazine Purple

Miscellaneous

3 Yds. of 4" Black Lace
5 Yds. of 1/4" Orange Ribbon
5 Yds. of 1/8" Purple Ribbon
1 Pot Belly #203
Liquitex Modeling Past
1-1/2 Yds of Black Cotton Fabric
12" Sq. of Fleshtone Felt
2 Packages of Red Curly Hair
1 Paper Mache Pumpkin
Loose Stuffing

Pumpkin

1. Base the pumpkin in Coral Rose. Wash a little Lemon Yellow down the center of each of the rises. Wash the entire pumpkin in Cadmium Orange
2. Float above all of the facial features with Lemon Yellow.
3. Base the eyes in White. Base all of the other facial features in Black. Do the stars in the eyes in White.

With the modeling paste stipple the centers of the spiders on her dress. For the mole on her nose take a small amount of modeling paste and roll it into a ball, flatten just a little bit. When dry glue to the gourd with tacky glue.

Witches Face

1. Base the gourd in Mocha. Float the shadows and wash the mole on her nose with Lt. Cinnamon.
2. Wash her cheeks and pink up the end of her nose with Gooseberry. Float the highlights on her face with White plus a touch of Gooseberry.
3. Base the inside of her mouth, nostrils, and eyebrows with Burnt Umber plus a touch of Black.
4. Base her teeth and eyes in White. Float the shadows on her teeth with Grey Sky.
5. Base her lips in Berry Red plus a touch of Gooseberry. Float the shadows with Berry Red plus a touch of Burnt Umber. Float the highlights with White plus a touch of Gooseberry.
6. Float the iris in her eyes in Mistletoe. Float a shadow under the upper lid with Black Forest plus a touch of Burnt Umber. Line eyes, do lashes and pupils all in Black. Highlight all facial features with White.
7. Base her dress entirely in Black.
8. Stipple the spider bodies wet in wet first with Lavender, then White to the upper half and Dioxazine Purple to the lower half. Do the legs in Heavy Metal Silver.
9. Paint the base in Dioxazine Purple.

Hat

You will need 2 circles 9" and 1 circle 12". With Wonder Under put the two 9" circles together. Cut the 12" circle in half and Wonder Under these two pieces together. Hot glue the half circle into a cone. Cut a 4" hole out of the center of the 9" circle. Glue the cone to the 9" circle.

Cape

The cape is a 18" x 24" rectangle. Use hot glue, hemming tape or sew a 1/2" hem on all 4 sides of the rectangle. Gather along one side of the 24". Hot glue purple ribbon over the gather.

Arms and Hands

The arms are a 24" x 9" rectangle. Hot glue along the 24" edge so that you end up with a long tube. Stuff the tube and gather 1" in from both ends. Do not gather this closed, leave an opening about 1-1/2" to slip in the hands. You will need 4 pieces of hands, hot glue these together and stuff. Hot glue into the ends of the arms. Hot glue these across her back and over the shoulders.

On the hat with the Heavy Metal Silver paint a spider web.

Twist the black lace, orange and purple ribbon all at one time around the pumpkin handle and on the hat. Make big fluffy bows with these three and hot glue to the hat and the pumpkin. Glue on hair and then hat.

Cut a hole in the bottom of the gourd 2" x 3/4" and slide down on the neck.

HAND OF FELT
CUT 4

SLIDES UP
INTO GOURD

GOURDIE NO SEW WITCH

BRING FABRIC
FOR ARMS UP OVER
THE SHOULDERS

15"
LONG

BASE IS CUT FROM 2" PINE
4" x 10"

LOVE AT
FIRST SIGHT

G092
G93
TRICK
OR
TREAT

WHICH ONE

PALETTE-Deco Americana

Berry Red
Moon Yellow
Burnt Sienna
Sand
Lemon Yellow
White
Mocha
Burnt Orange
Raw Sienna
Gooseberry
Uniform Blue
Mink Tan
Black
Pumpkin
Burnt Umber
Sapphire
Light Cinnamon

Miscellaneous

3 Florist Leaves
Green Florist Wire
Teal Paper Twist
Jute
3" Each of Red, Blue, and Yellow 1/8" Ribbon

1. Wash the pumpkin in Pumpkin. Float the shadows first with Burnt Orange and then Burnt Sienna. Base the inside of the nose, mouth and eyes in Moon Yellow plus a touch of Lemon Yellow. Shade with Raw Sienna. Fill in the dark areas with Light Cinnamon and line with Black.
2. Base all of the flesh areas in Mocha on the clown. Float the shadows with Light Cinnamon. Wash little touches of pink on all of the areas with Gooseberry. Base the eyes and the mouth area in White. Base the hearts and his nose in Berry Red. Shade the red areas with Burnt Sienna. Base the iris of the eye in Sapphire, do the lashes and the pupil in Black.
3, Base his shirt in Sand. Do the plaid in a wide stripe of Berry Red and a narrow stripe of Sapphire Blue. Float all of the shadows on the shirt with Light Cinnamon. Float the highlights with White.
4. Base the pants in Uniform Blue. Float the shadows with Uniform Blue plus a touch of Black. Float the highlights and do the strings around the holes with White plus a touch of Uniform Blue.
5. Base his hair in Moon Yellow. Stipple the highlights with Lemon Yellow and then White. Float the shadows with Burnt Sienna.
6. Base the stem and the soles of his shoes in Burnt Umber. Float the shadows with Black and the highlights with Mocha.
7, Base the tie and the buttons on the suspenders in Berry Red. Float the shadows with Berry Red plus a touch of Black and the highlights with Gooseberry.
8. Base in all of the black areas and highlight them with White plus a touch of Black.

Bear Mask

Base the bear in Sand plus Raw Sienna. Float the shadows with Burnt Sienna. Stipple the highlights with Sand. Float the muzzle and the inside of the ears with Gooseberry. Do all of the facial features in Black. Highlight with White.

Trick or Treat

Wash the board with Mink Tan. Float the shadows and do the lines in the boards with Burnt Umber. Do the lettering and all of the eyes and mouths in Black. Line the tops of the mouths and dot the eyes with Sand.

Boxer Mask

Base the entire mask in Mocha. Float the cheeks with Gooseberry. Float the shadow with Light Cinnamon and the highlights with White plus a touch of Mocha. Wash the bruises with Uniform Blue and Purple. Outline all with Burnt Umber. Do eyebrows and hair in Black.

The bush is small pieces of torn paper twist hot glued in place. They are torn so they will have rough edges.

BUSH IS CUT FROM 1/4" BIRCH
THE CLOWN & PUMPKIN, ONE FOOT, ONE ARM, AND TRICK OR TREAT SIGN ARE 1/2" PINE.
ALL MASKS AND HATS ARE 1/4" BIRCH
MASKS ARE DRILLED FOR EYES
WOOD AVAILABLE THROUGH:
THE LACE PLACE.
WHICH ONE

WOOD AVAILABLE:
TODD HUPP

NOAH'S ARK

NOAH'S ARK

PALETTE-Deco Art Americana

Antique Gold
Mocha
Burnt Umber
Sand
Grey Sky
White
Light Cinnamon
Burnt Sienna
Raw Sienna
French Blue Grey
Uniform Blue
Black
Moon Yellow
Country Red
Slate Grey
Gooseberry

ARK

1. Wash the ark in Sand plus a touch of Burnt Umber. Add a little more Burnt Umber to this and wash the deck, ramp and float the shadows under all of the boards. Float the highlight on the boards with White.
2. Base the wheels in Grey Sky Float around the inside near the hub with Slate Grey.
3. Wash all of the windows, doors, and portholes with French Blue Grey. Float the darker shadows in these areas with French Blue Grey.
4. Base all of the areas to be red in Sand. Wash over this with Country Red. Float the shadows with Country Red plus Burnt Sienna. Float the highlights with Sand plus a touch of Country Red.

ZEBRA

Base the zebra in White plus a touch of Grey Sky. Float the shadows with Slate Grey. Do the stripes and the mane in Black. Highlight the mane with a few White strokes.

ELEPHANT AND HIPPO

1. Base the lions face in a mix of Raw Sienna plus a touch of Sand. Float the shadows with Light Cinnamon. Float the highlights with Moon Yellow.
2. Float around the head to make the mane with Burnt Umber. With a grainier draw in towards the head from the outside of the mane first with Moon Yellow and then with White.

GIRAFFE

1. Base the giraffe in Moon Yellow plus a touch of Antique Gold. Float the shadows with Light Cinnamon.
2. Do the spots in Burnt Umber plus a touch of Black. Also do the mane and the tail with this mix. Stroke highlights on the mane and tail with Sand.

MONKEY'S

1. Base the monkeys in Light Cinnamon. Float the shadows with Burnt Umber. Float the highlights in Moon Yellow plus a touch of Sand.
2. Base the banana in Moon Yellow.
3. Base their faces and ears in Mocha. Float the shadows on these areas with Light Cinnamon.

WALRUS

1. Base in Slate Grey plus a touch of Black. Float the shadows with Black. Float the highlights with Grey Sky. Do the whiskers with strokes of Grey Sky.
2. Base the tusks in White plus a touch of Sand. Float the shadow with Light Cinnamon.

To finish float all of the noses, cheeks and inside of the ears with Gooseberry. Do all eyes and line everything with Black. Highlight the eyes with just a little touch of blue and then a little touch of White.

PLANTER WAGON

PALETTE-Deco Americana

Black	Lavender	Blue Haze
Light Cinnamon	Boysenberry	Moon Yellow
Cashmere Beige	White	Cranberry Wine
Crimson Tide	Dioxazine Purple	Jade Green

Base all the pieces of the wagon in White plus a touch of Cashmere Beige.

1. Pat the background all around the flowers and berries and under the leaves first with Jade Green. The darker areas under the roses are then patted with Dark Pine plus a touch of Black.
2. With a #6 filbert stroke in all of the green leaves with a mix of Jade Green and Dark Pine. Float the shadows on the lower half of the leaves with Dark Pine plus a touch of Black. Stroke the little blue shadow leaves in with the filbert and Blue Haze plus a touch of White.
3. Do all of the stems and the twigs in Light Cinnamon.
4. Wash the berries in with a mix of 1/2 Lavender and 1/2 Boysenberry. Float the lower half of the berry in a mix of Dioxazine Purple and Cranberry Wine. Float the upper half with Crimson Tide. Float all of the highlights on the berries with White plus a touch of Lavender.
5. Base the roses in Boysenberry plus a touch of White. Float along the bottom edge of the rose and the inside of the bowl with Crimson Tide. Float the deeper shadows inside the bowl again with Cranberry Wine. Float all of the petals in White with the filbert. Stipple the inside of the roses with Moon Yellow.
6. Do all of the small hearts and wash the shadows on the roses with Blue Haze plus a touch of White.
7. Do all of the accent dots with White.
8. Wash the inside of the wheel with Lavender and Boysenberry. Float with Blue Haze.
9. Do all of the banding with Dark Pine plus a touch of Black.

PLANTER WAGON

BACK

G©93

FRONT

G©93

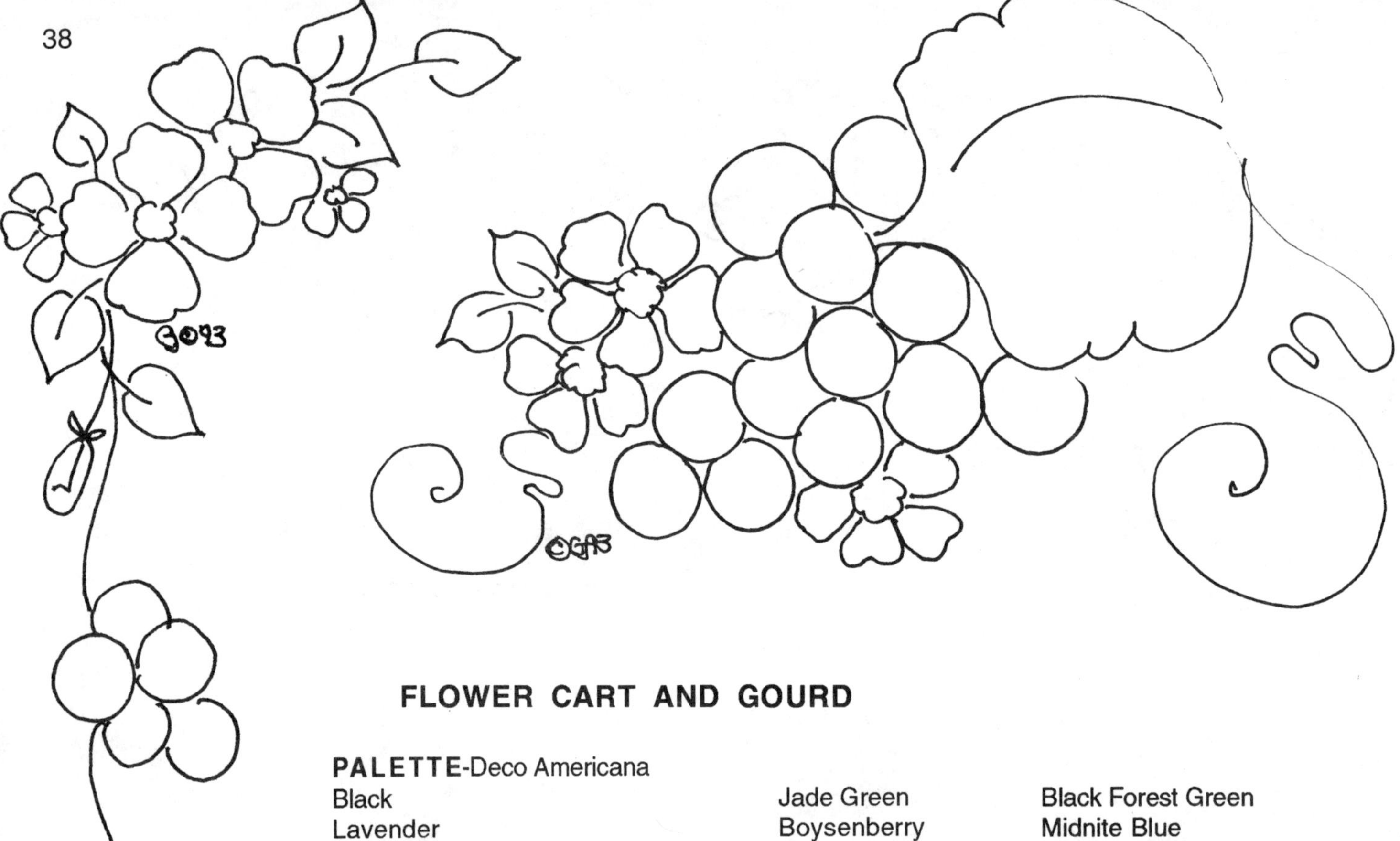

FLOWER CART AND GOURD

PALETTE-Deco Americana

Black
Lavender
Cranberry Wine
Raw Sienna
French Blue Grey
Jade Green
Boysenberry
Moon Yellow
Forest Green
Mauve
Black Forest Green
Midnite Blue
Dioxazine Purple
Snow White

The two base colors for the cart I mixed in a bottle because you will need so much of them. One is a bottle of Cranberry Wine with about a teaspoon of Midnight Blue. The other is a bottle of Midnite Blue with about 2 teaspoons of Black. According to the color picture base in the entire cart. Band all of this with White plus a touch of the dark blue mix.

The flowers on these two pieces are done with one or 2 strokes and only one coat of paint. If a little of the background color shows through it will be all right.

Leaves

With Forest Green and a #4 or #8 filbert depending on the size of the leaf stroke in all leaves. Float a shadow on the bottom of the leaves with Black Forest Green. Float a highlight on the leaves and do all stems and tole strokes with Jade Green.

Grapes

With a #4 filbert fill in each individual grape with a mix of 1/2 Lavender and 1/2 Mauve. Float the shadows with a mix of Dioxazine Purple plus a touch of the dark blue mix. Float the highlights with White plus a touch of Lavender. Do the little liner highlights with White plus a touch of Mauve.

Pink Flowers

These flowers will take 2 strokes with a #8 filbert to fill in. Stroke these in with a mix of 1/2 Mauve and 1/2 Boysenberry. The buds are done with one stroke. Float the shadows with dark burgundy mix. Float the highlights with White plus a touch of Boysenberry.

Blue Flowers

With a #4 filbert stroke in these small blue flowers with French Blue Grey. Float the shadows on these with the dark blue mix. Float the highlights with White plus a touch of the dark blue mix.

Yellow Flowers

With a #4 filbert stroke in these small yellow flowers with Moon Yellow. Float the shadows with Raw Sienna and the highlights with White plus a touch of Moon Yellow.

Stipple the centers of all flowers wet in wet, first with Moon Yellow, then the bottom edge with Raw Sienna and the upper edge with White.

SANTA CLAUS
PAGES 54, 55
A CHRISTMAS BIRD HOUSE
FOR EVERYONE
CANDY CANE COW
PAGES 54, 55
LARGE HEART
PAGE 55
CHRISTMAS TREE
PAGES 54, 55
ROSE STOCKING
PAGES 54, 55
SMALL HEART
PAGE 55
PEGUIN CANDY CANE
PAGES 54, 55
Noël!

MOM'S FAVORITE
PAGES 47, 50, 51

HOG HEAVEN
PAGES 18, 19

SUNNY AND WARM
PAGES 23, 24, 25

BELLA COW
PAGES 13, 14, 15

FUNKY BUNNY AND EGG
PAGES 52, 53

LITTLE CHILD ROBE RACK
PAGES 20, 21, 22

STRUTTIN
PAGES 70, 72, 73

MOM'S FAVORITES
Recipe Box, Filter Box, Pot Holder

PALETTE-Deco Americana

Black
French Blue Grey
Boysenberry
Raspberry
Cranberry Wine
Slate Grey
Dioxazine Purple
Fleshtone
Blueberry
Light Cinnamon
Country Blue
Sand
Salem Blue
Mauve
Black Forest Green
Gooseberry
Buttermilk
Raw Sienna
Deep Teal
White
Brush n Blend

1. Base the cat, bottom of coffee filter box, and all of the recipe box except for he lid in French Blue Grey. Mix 2 :Deep Teal, 1:Black Forest Green with some Brush n Blend mixed into this, streak all of the areas that you based in blue.
2. Base the lid and the coffee filter lid in 1/2 Buttermilk and 1/2 White mix. Pat around the edges of these two pieces first with a little Raspberry, then a little Blueberry, and last quite a bit more of the dark green mix. All of the solid green edges are done with the dark green mix also. When all of this is completed do the narrow pink banding in a mix of 1/2 Boysenberry and 1/2 Mauve.

Little Girl

1. Base her dress in White plus a touch of Mauve. Float all of the shadows first with Raspberry and then the darker ones with Cranberry Wine. Float the highlights with White plus a touch of Boysenberry.
2. Wash her pinafore with White. Float the highlights with White. Float the shadows lightly with Blueberry plus a touch of Slate Grey.
3. Base all of the skin areas in Fleshtone. Float the shadows first with Light Cinnamon, then float over the darker ones again with the same color. Wash all of the pink areas on her skin with Gooseberry. Base her lips in a mix of Gooseberry plus a touch of Raspberry. Highlight all of these areas with White plus a touch of Fleshtone.
4. Base her eyes in White. Float the iris in Blueberry. Float under the upper eyelid with Blueberry plus a touch of Slate Grey. Do the lashes and pupils in Black.
5. Base her hair in Raw Sienna plus a touch of Sand. Float the shadows on this with Burnt Umber. With a grainier streak in the dark hairs with Burnt Umber and the highlights with Sand.
6. Base the beater in Slate Grey. Shade with Black and highlight with White. Base the frosting in Burnt Umber plus a touch of Sand. Shade with Burnt Umber, highlight Sand.

Flowers and Leaves For All Pieces

A #4 filbert is used for all the flowers and the leaves.

1. Stroke the pink flowers in the banding mix. Float the shadows with Raspberry and the highlights with White plus a touch of Boysenberry.
2. For the lavender flowers stroke in Country Blue. Float the shadows with Dioxazine Purple plus a touch of Blueberry. Float the highlights with White plus a touch of Country Blue.
3. For the blue flowers stroke in Salem Blue. Float the shadows with Blueberry and the highlights with White plus a touch of Blueberry.
4. Stroke the leaves in the dark mix from the edging. Highlight and do the stems in Deep Teal plus a touch of White.
5. Stipple the centers of all of the flowers with Raw Sienna and White.

½ OF GOURD
CONNECT AT ✱
SIDE OF C
ROOF OF CART

POT BELLY GOURD #PB 203
AND FLOWER CART
AVAILABLE! STAN BROWNS

FLOWER CART AND GOURD

MOM
FAVORI
©G93
FILTER BOX
SIDE REPEAT
ALL THE WAY AROUND
©G93

MOM'S FAVORITES
Recipe Box, Filter Box, Pot Holder

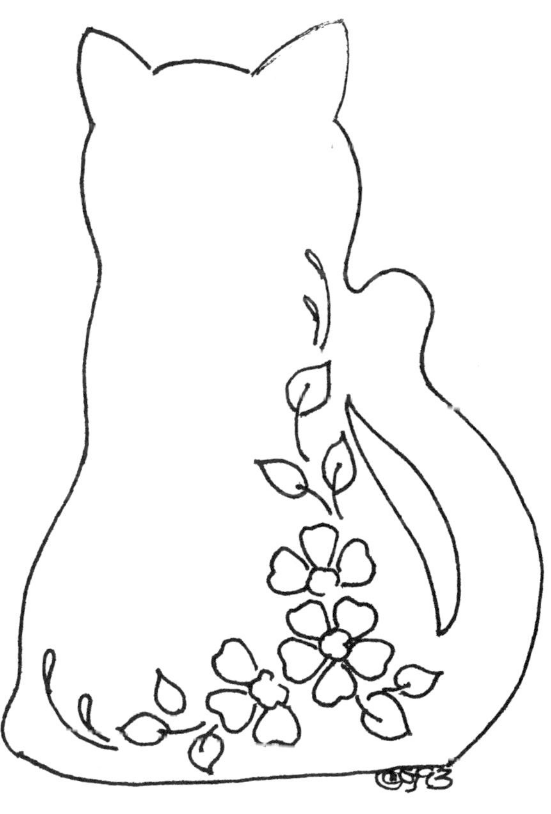

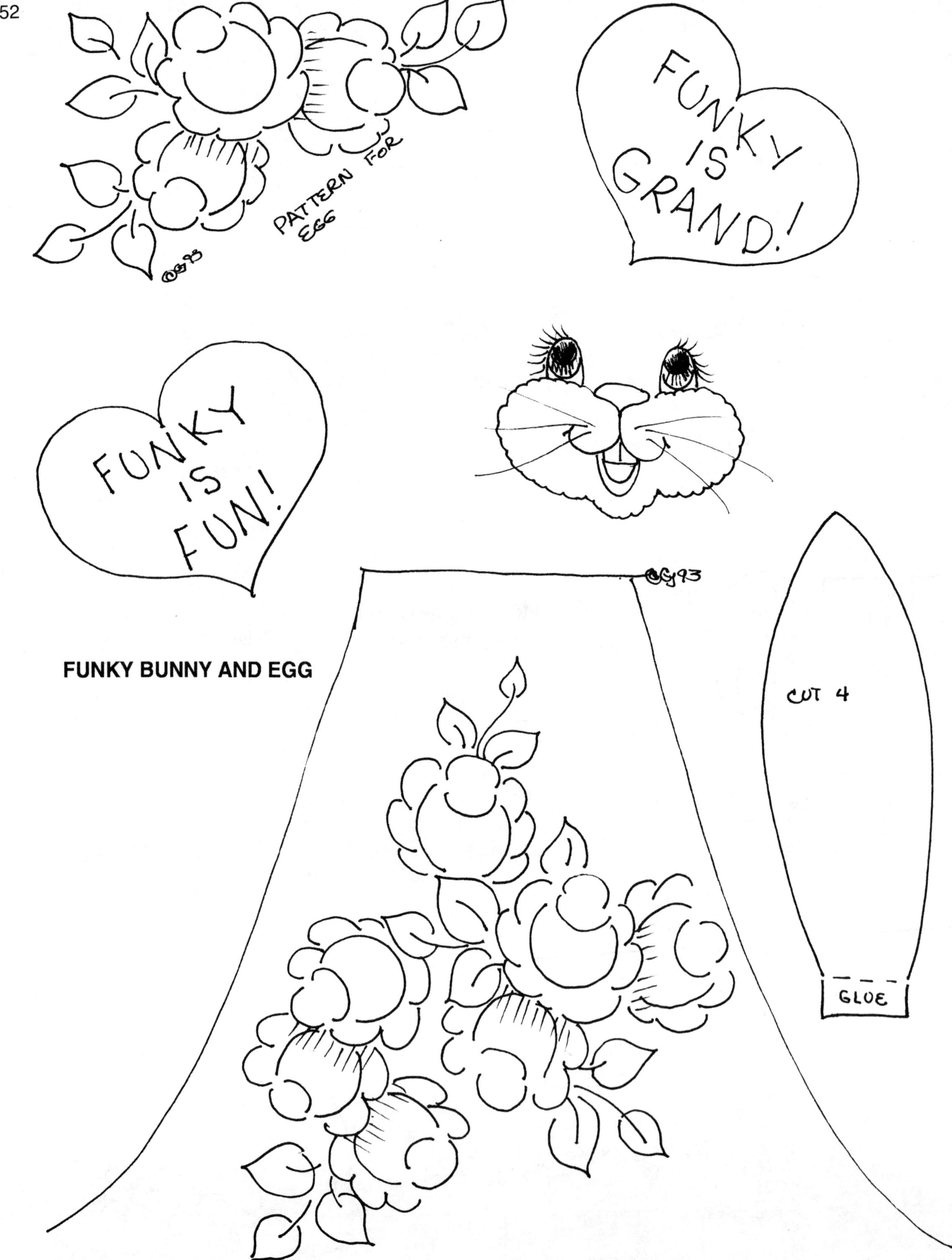

FUNKY BUNNY AND EGG

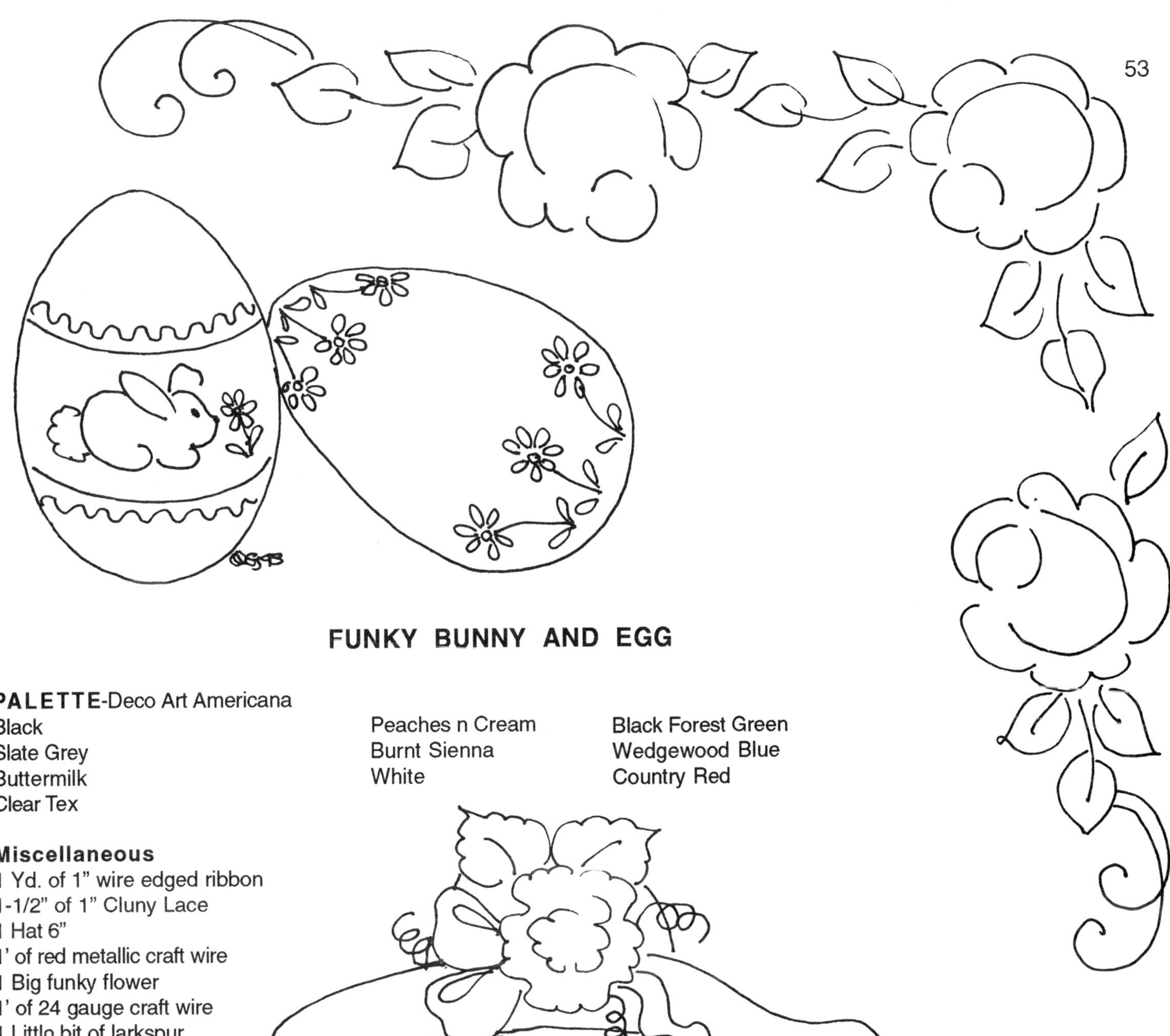

FUNKY BUNNY AND EGG

PALETTE-Deco Art Americana

Black
Slate Grey
Buttermilk
Clear Tex
Peaches n Cream
Burnt Sienna
White
Black Forest Green
Wedgewood Blue
Country Red

Miscellaneous

1 Yd. of 1" wire edged ribbon
1-1/2" of 1" Cluny Lace
1 Hat 6"
1' of red metallic craft wire
1 Big funky flower
1' of 24 gauge craft wire
1 Littlo bit of larkspur
1 Bowling pin 9"
1 Egg 4"

1. Base the panel on her dress and the egg in Buttermilk.
2. Base the peach area on her dress and pat in all of the light roses on both with Peaches n Cream. Paint in the darker roses with a mix of 1/2 Peaches n Cream and 1/2 Country Red. Pat in the darkest roses in Country Red. Float the shadows around the edge of the dress and the bowl of the light roses in Country Red. Float the highlight on these two with White (petal on roses). Float the shadows on the middle roses with Country Red plus a touch of Burnt Sienna. Float the petals on these with White plus a touch of Peaches n Cream. Float the shadows on the darker roses with Burnt Sienna plus a touch of Country Red. Float the petals on these with Peaches n Cream.
3. Wash around all of the roses with a mix of Wedgewood Blue plus a touch of Black Forest Green. Stroke the leaves with this color with a #8 filbert.
4. Base the bunnies face in White plus a touch of Slate Grey. Float the shadows with Slate Grey. Mix a little Clear Tex in with White and stipple the highlights on her face.
5. Float the cheeks, nose and the mouth with Peaches n Cream plus a touch of Country Red.
6. Float the eyes in White. Float the iris with Wedgewood Blue. Do the pupils, lashes and line all of the facial features with Black. Highlight all of the facial features with White.

To Make Ears:

Cut 4 pieces of ears out of White fabric. Cut a piece of the 24 gauge wire the length of the ear. Lay this down through the center and Wonder Under the 2 pieces together. This enables you to bend and twist the ears.

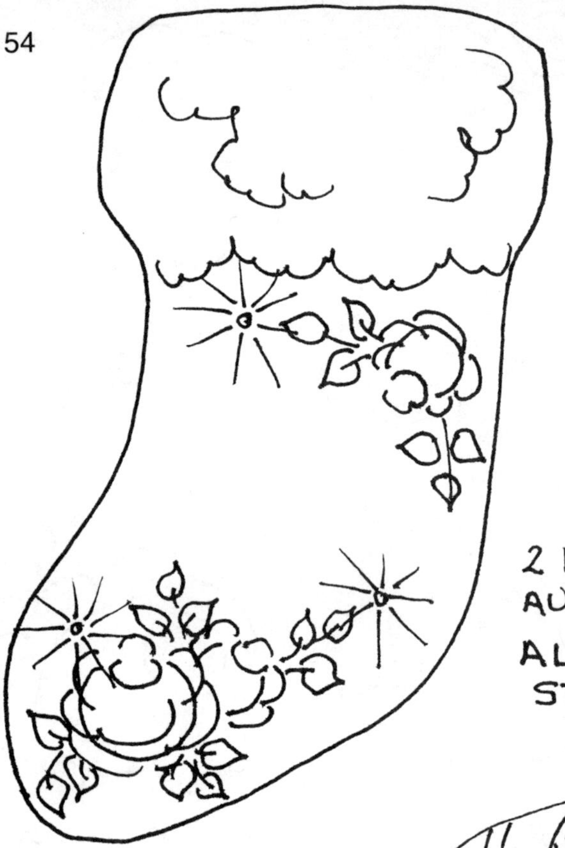

2 HEART SHAPED BIRD HOUSES AVAILABLE: PLUM FUN

ALL OTHERS AVAILABLE: STAN BROWN'S

A CHRISTMAS BIRD HOUSE FOR EVERYONE

PALETTE-Deco Americana

Black
Mauve
Cranberry Wine
Sand
Gooseberry

Light Cinnamon
Calico Red
Moon Yellow
Dark Pine
White

Blueberry
Mocha
Crimson Tide
Terra Cotta

Penguin Candy Cane

1. Base the entire candy cane in White. Float the stripes with Calico Red and line with Crimson Tide. Do thin lines with Dark Pine.
2. Do the feet and the beaks in Terra Cotta, highlight with Moon Yellow.
3. Do the penguins in Black.

Candy Cane Cow

1. Base he entire candy cane in White.
2. Wash the bow with Calico Red, and float the shadows with Crimson Tide.
3. Wash the nose, ears and udder in Mocha, float the shadow with Light Cinnamon, float the pink areas with Gooseberry, and highlight with White.
4. Do the hooves and float the shadows with White plus a touch of Black.
5. Do all of the spots in Black. Dot the eyes with Blueberry plus White and highlight White.

Rose Stocking

1. Base the stocking part in Blueberry.
2. Stipple the upper part wet in wet first Mauve, then Cranberry Wine and last White.
3. Pat the rose with Mauve. Float the shadows with Cranberry Wine. Float the petals with White plus a touch of Calico Red.
4. Float around the roses with Black Forest Green. Stroke the leaves with Dark Pine plus a touch of White.
5. The dots are Sand and the stars are White.

Christmas Tree

1. Base the tree in Dark Pine. Float the shadows with Black Forest Green and the highlights with White plus a touch of Dark Pine.
2. Do the dots in Calico Red. Do the bows in White plus a touch of Calico Red. Do the stars in White.

Santa Claus

1. Base the lower half of the stocking in Calico Red. Float the shadows around the beard in Cranberry Wine.
2. Base the face in Mocha and float the cheeks with Gooseberry. Dot the nose with Calico Red and the eyes with Black. Highlight all of the features with White.
3. Base all of the hair areas in White plus a touch of Black. Float the shadows with Black. With a grainier streak in the white hair.
4. Stipple the upper part of the stocking wet in wet Blueberry and then White.

Large Heart

1. Base the house in Calico Red and the roof in Dark Pine.
2. Stipple all of the greenery wet in wet Black Forest Green and then White.
3. Dot the berries first with Gooseberry and then more with White plus a touch of Blueberry.
4. Do the bows in Sand.

Small Heart

1. Base the house in Blueberry and the roof in White plus a touch of Blueberry.
2. Stipple all of the greenery wet in wet first with Dark Pine and then with White.
3. Dot the berries and do the lettering all in Calico Red.

Spatter all of the bird houses with White.

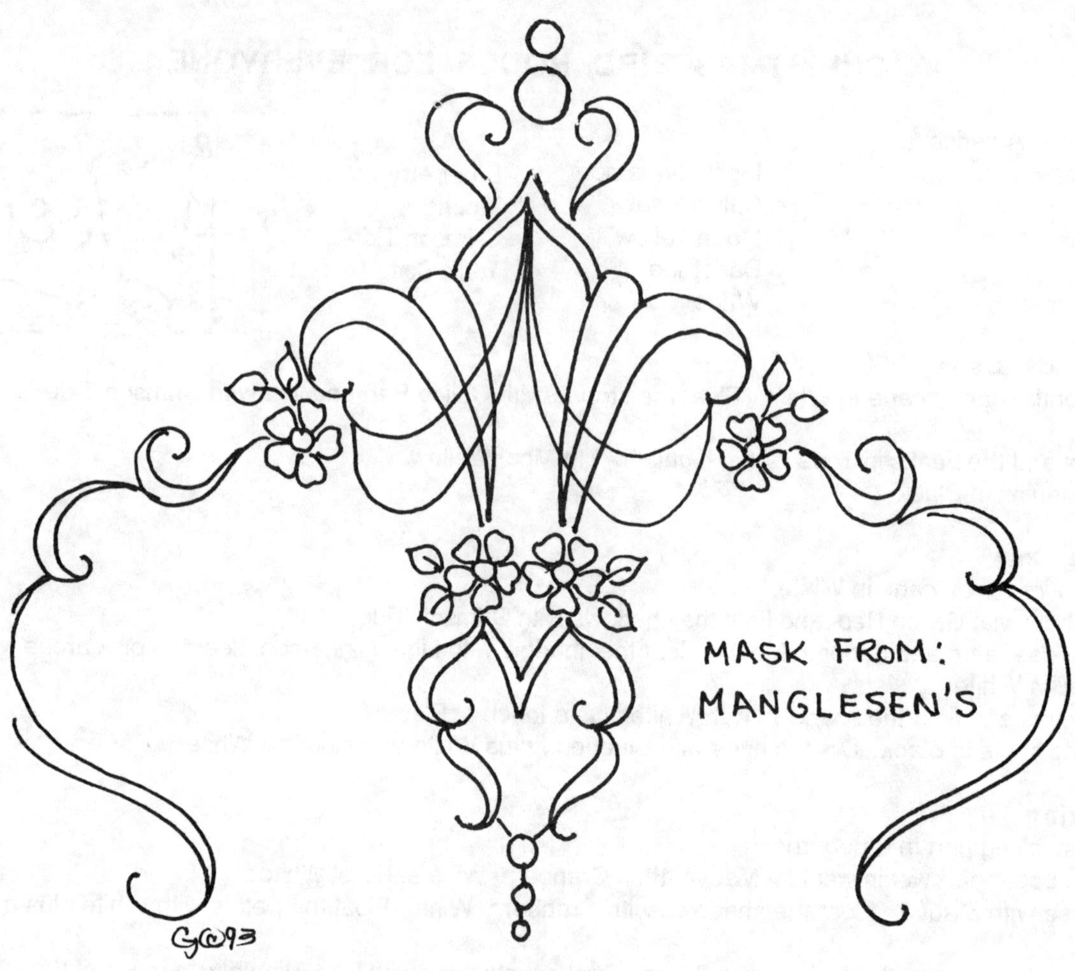

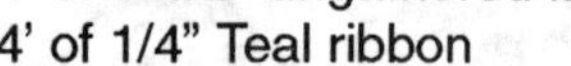

MASK

PALETTE -Deco Art Americana

Black Forest Green
Burnt Umber
Buttermilk
Crimson Tide
Glorious Gold
White
Mauve
Grey Sky

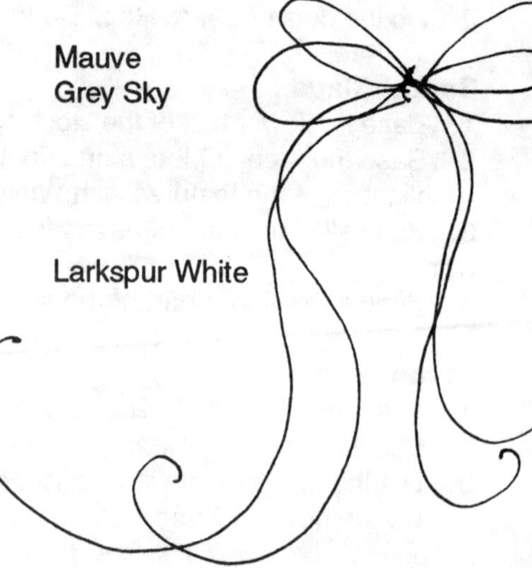

Miscellaneous Supplies:

Dried Flowers:

Dusty Rose Caspia
Eucalyptus Dark Green
German Statice Neutral
Star Dust Gyp
Larkspur White

Lace

2-1/2 Yds. of 1-1/4" Gathered Lace
4' of 1-1/2" ungathered lace
4' of 1/4" Teal ribbon
1-1/2' of Pearls

1. Base the mask in a mix of of 1/2 Buttermilk and 1/2 White.
2. Float above the eye slits with Black Forest Green.
3. Float the lips first with Mauve and then with Mauve plus a touch of Crimson Tide.
4. Float under the gold mask with a mix of Grey Sky plus a touch of Burnt Umber.
5. Base the gold areas all in Glorious Gold. Float all of the shadows on these areas and line everything with Burnt Umber.

All of the dried flowers are hot glued to the side of the mask. Truthfully I've never had any instruction in flowers so this probably isn't proper, but it worked for me.

HOUSEWORK MAKES ME CRAZY
AND
HEN PARTY

PALETTE-Deco Art American

Black
Buttermilk
Terra Cotta
Light Cinnamon
Moon Yellow
Rookwood Red
Grey Sky
White
Uniform Blue
Country Red
Toffee

Miscellaneous: Blue jean scraps for the legs

1. Wash the main board with Toffee. Wash the squares in Rookwood Red.
2. Base all of the chickens with Buttermilk. Float the shadows with Light Cinnamon and float the highlights with White.
3. Base the blue jeans in Grey Sky. With a mix of Uniform Blue plus a touch of Black stipple all over the jeans with a sponge. Float the shadows with this mix and the highlights with Uniform Blue plus White.
4. Wash the waddle, comb, and the cheeks in Country Red. Float the shadows with Rookwood Red and float the highlights with Moon Yellow plus a touch of Country Red. Use this mix to do the stitching on the pants.
5. Base the feet and the beak in Terra Cotta. Float the highlights with Moon Yellow.
6. Do all of the outlining and the eyes in Black. Put a little blue in the eyes and a White highlight.
7. Spatter with Black.

HOUSEWORK
MAKES ME
CRA-A-AZY!
©93G

YAK!
YAK!
YAK!
CHICKENS 3/4" PINE
AVAILABLE: THE
LACE PLACE

©9BS
HAND THROWN POTTERY
AVAILABLE: ROD BENNETT
APPLY THIS HALF OF PATTERN FIRST AND DO ALL PAINTING THEN APPLY REST OF PATTERN.
©9BS

ONION KEEPER AND GARLIC KEEPER

These beautiful hand thrown pots are done by Rod Bennett. Rod minored in pottery at Eastern Oregon State College, and is a professional potter, but alas he has turned into a computer and science teacher. What a waste of a good talent. I can get away with saying that because he's my brother. Each pot is individually thrown on a potter's wheel therefore they may vary slightly in size or shape. They are drilled in the bottom lip and the lid fits slightly loose so that the pot can breath. This keeps your onions rotting. The insides of all pots are glazed but because of the acrylic on the outside it is not recommended that you submerse them in dish water. Just sponge them off. For pricing contact Rod Bennett, Wagon Wheel Pottery, P. O. Box 782, Crane, Or. 97732, (503) 493-2744.

PALETTE-Deco Art Americana

Antique Gold
French Blue Grey
Burnt Umber
Uniform Blue
Country Red
Forest Green
Burnt Sienna
Slate Grey
Cadmium Orange
White
Black
Plantation Pine
Buttermilk
Terra Cotta

Miscellaneous

Brush n Blend
Saran Wrap

Base all of the blue areas in a mix of White plus French Blue Grey. You will need a mix of Uniform Blue plus a touch of Black, to this mix add an equal amount of Brush n Blend. Work only one area at a time. Cover the light blue with the dark blue. Lay a sheet of Saran Wrap over this, push on the Saran Wrap here and there and then lift. Base the center of the onion keeper and the veggies on the garlic pot all in Buttermilk. Float around the edges of the large pot in Burnt Umber plus a touch of Buttermilk. All of the dark blue banding is done in Uniform Blue and Black mix.

1. Wash the jalapeno pepper in Plantation Pine plus a touch of Buttermilk. Float the shadows on these with Plantation Pine. Float the highlights with White plus a touch of Antique Gold. Touch around the base of the stem where it connects with the pepper with Burnt Sienna.
2. Wash the tomato in Cadmium Orange. Wash over this with Country Red. Float the shadows with Country Red plus a touch of Burnt Sienna. Float the highlights with White plus a touch of Cadmium Orange. Do the stem in a wash of Plantation Pine. Float the shadows with the same and the highlights with White plus a touch of Antique Gold.
3. Wash the green onions in White. Float the shadows on these with Slate Grey plus a touch of Burnt Sienna. Wash the green sections with Forest Green, drag a little of this down onto the White areas. Float the shadows on these areas with Forest Green.
4. Wash the green peppers in Forest Green, float the shadows with the same. Float the highlights with White plus a touch of Forest Green.

Put on the pattern for the remaining veggies and the basket.

1. Do the wire on the basket with Slate Grey. Float the shadows with Slate Grey plus Black, and the highlights with White. Wash the handle in Burnt Umber. Float the shadows with the same. Float the highlights with Buttermilk.
2. Wash the onions with Terra Cotta. Float the shadows first with Terra Cotta and then with Burnt Sienna. Wash the highlights with White plus a touch of Antique Gold.
3. Wash the hot peppers on both pieces with Country Red. Float the shadows with Burnt Sienna. Float the highlights with White plus a touch of Terra Cotta. Do the stems in Terra Cotta plus a touch of Plantation Pine. Float shadows on stems with Burnt Umber, highlight White plus Antique Gold.
4. Do the green onion down front the same as the one in the basket.
5. Wash the garlic in Buttermilk plus a tiny touch of Burnt Umber. Float the shadows with Slate Grey plus a touch of Burnt Umber. Float the highlights with White.
6. Line everything and spatter the veggies with Black.

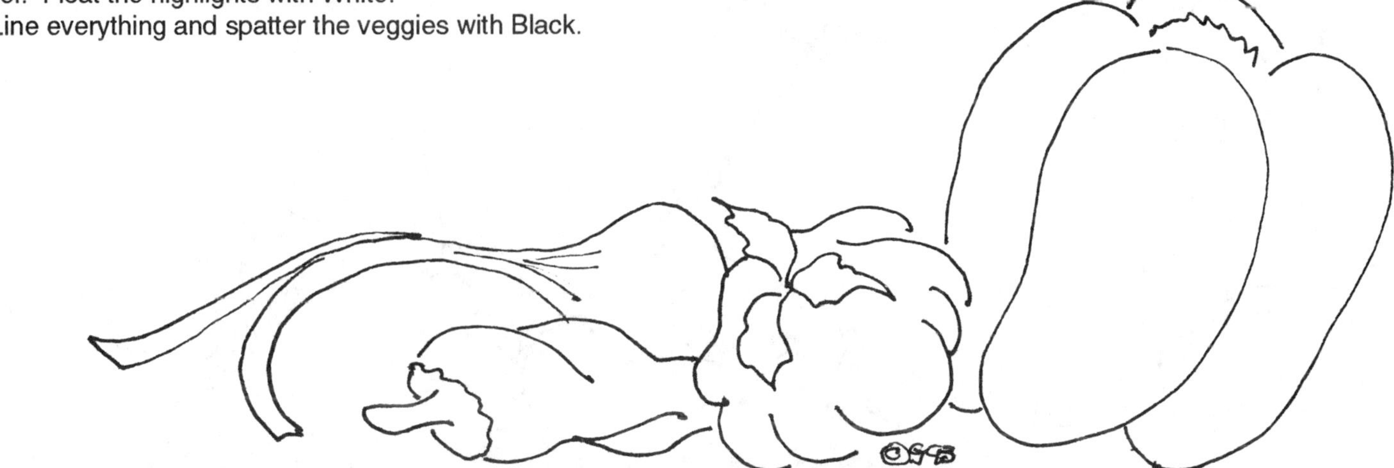

BLESS THIS HOME AND BASKET

PALETTE-Deco Americana

Burnt Sienna
Moon Yellow
Country Red
Salem Blue
Forest Green
Wedgewood Blue
Lemon Yellow
Midnite Blue
Black Forest Green
Russet
Dioxazine Purple
Warm Neutral Toning
Lavender
Brush n Blend Medium
Buttermilk
Plantation Pine
Deep Teal
Terra Cotta
Gooseberry
White

Miscellaneous

Liquitex Modeling Paste
Palette Knife

With a palette knife and the modeling paste texture the ends of the basket and the blessings board. I followed the directions on the bottle and it worked really well.

1. Base all of the textured areas in Buttermilk. With a mix of Brush n Blend, and Warm Neutral Toning antique the textured areas.
2. With a mix of 1/2 Wedgewood Blue and 1/2 Black Forest Green do all of the dark areas on the basket, all banding, and lettering. All of the thin banding is a mix of 1/2 White and 1/2 Raw Sienna

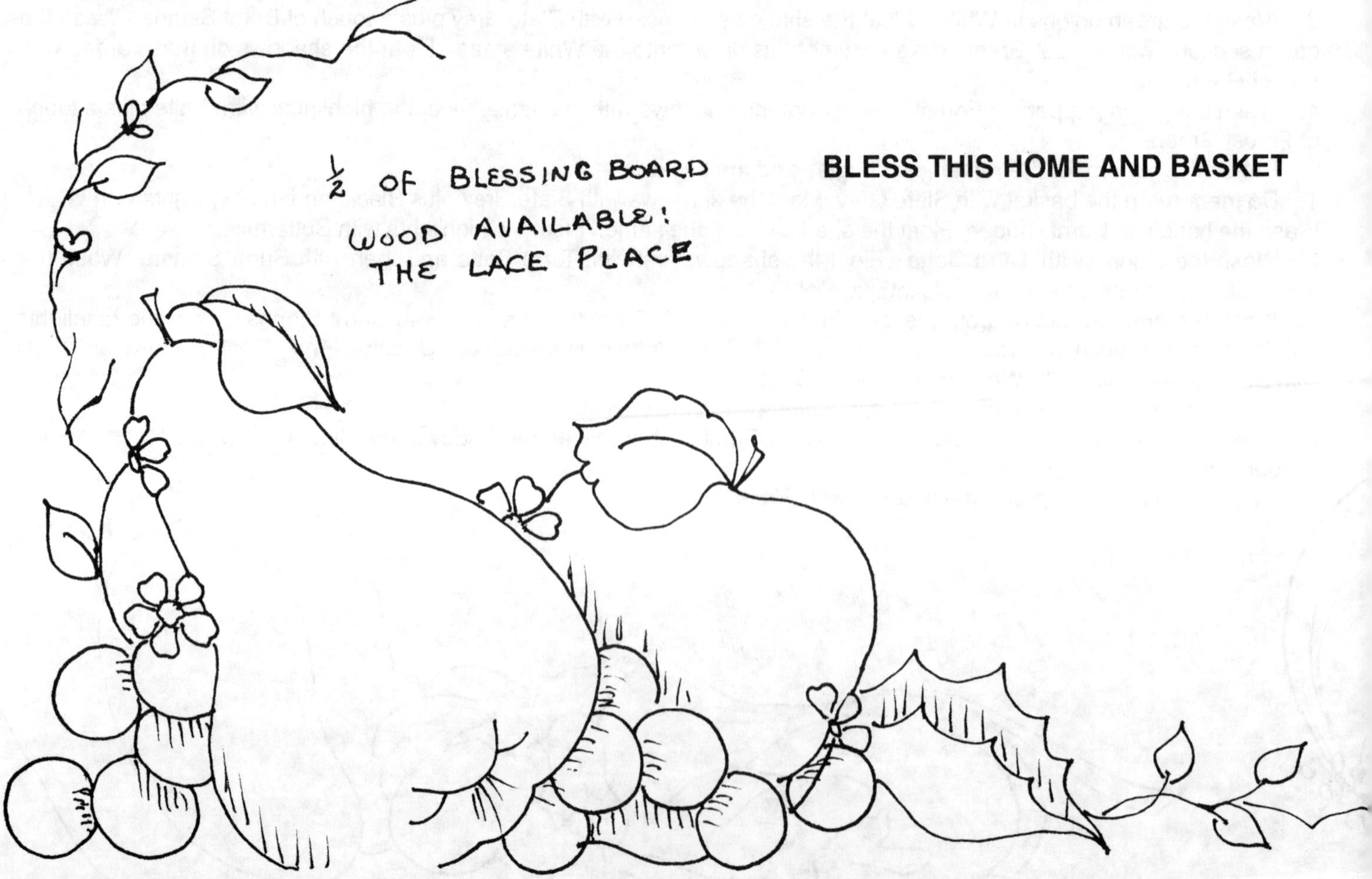

1/2 OF BLESSING BOARD
WOOD AVAILABLE!
THE LACE PLACE

BLESS THIS HOME AND BASKET

3. Base the apples in Gooseberry. Wash with Country Red. Float the highlight in Country Red plus White. Float the shadows first with Country Red and then the darker shadows with Russet. Float in the center of the highlight area with White.

4. Base the pears in Moon Yellow plus a touch of Terra Cotta. Float the highlights first with Moon Yellow plus White. Float the shadows first with Terra Cotta, and then the darker ones with Burnt Sienna. Wash the highlight areas with a little Lemon Yellow.

5. Base the grapes in Lavender. Float the shadows with Dioxazine Purple plus a touch of Midnite Blue. Float the highlights with White plus a touch of Lavender. The brightest is White plus a touch of the shadow mix.

6. Base all of the leaves in Forest Green plus a touch of Warm Neutral Toning. Float the shadows on the olive colored leaves with Plantation Pine. Add a little White to this and float the brightest highlights. Float the shadows on the bluer leaves with Deep Teal. Float the highlights with Salem Blue.

7. With a #4 filbert brush stroke in the flower petals with a mix of White plus a touch of Gooseberry. Very lightly float the shadows on these with Country Red. Float the highlights with White.

8. Do all of the stems and branches with Russet.

but the fruit of
Spirit
love,
pe

ALL PIECES
ARE CUT FROM
3/4" PINE WOOD
AVAILABLE THE LACE
PLACE

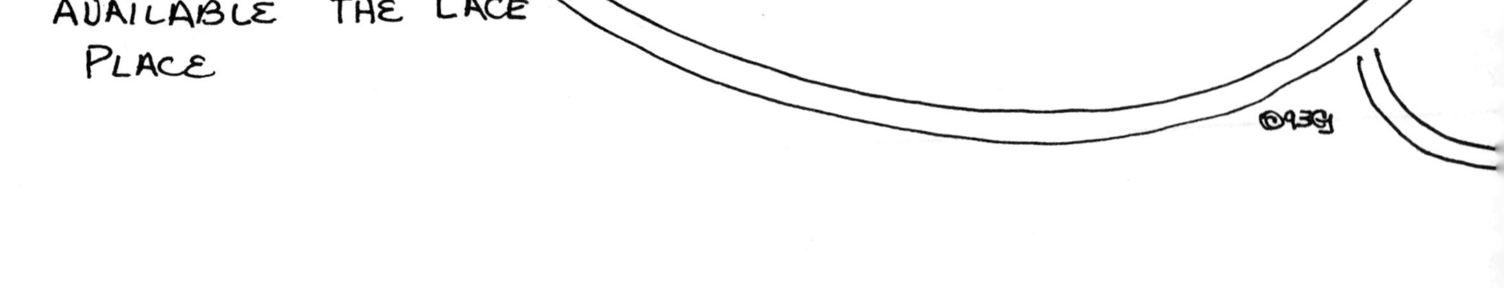

WATERMELON

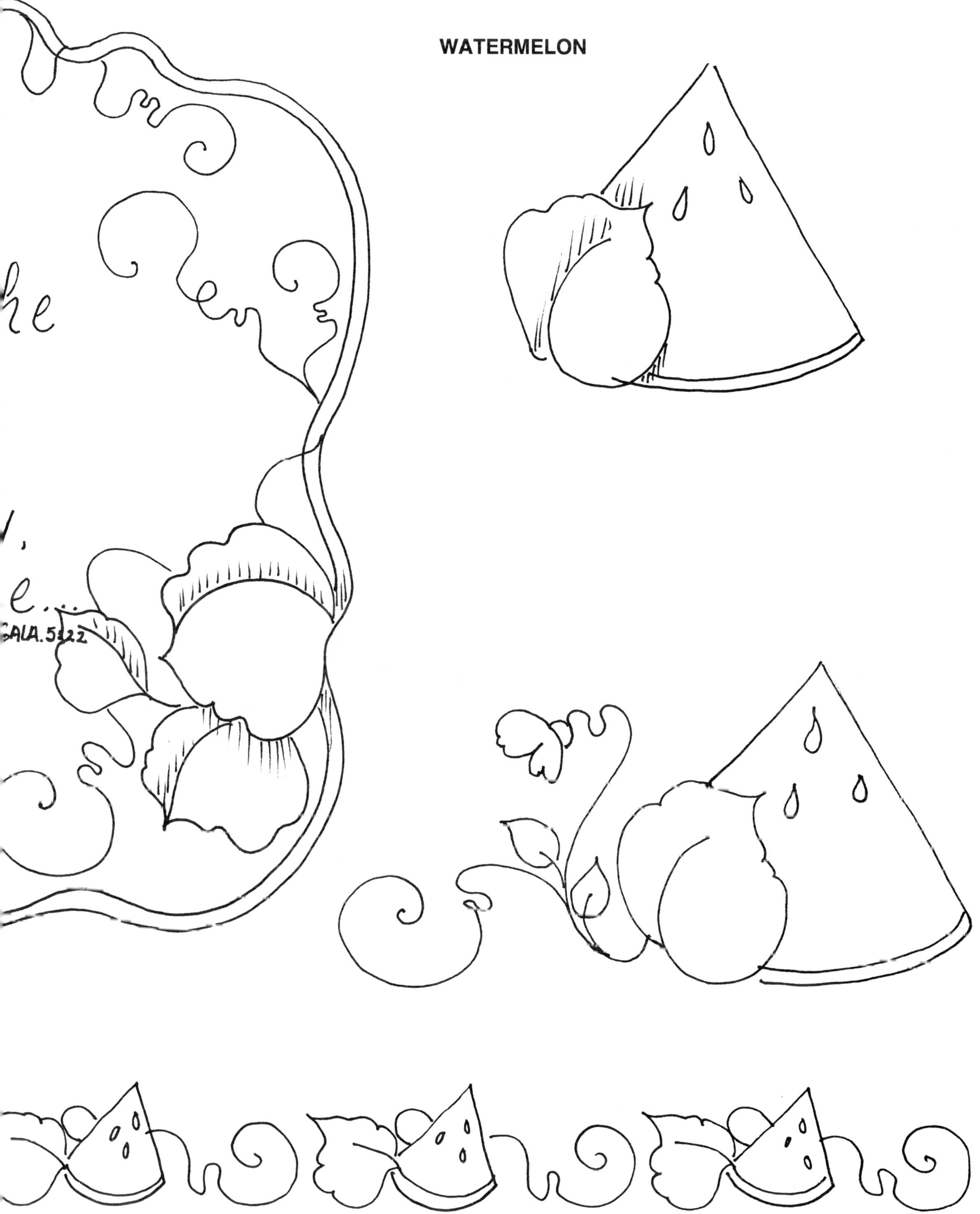

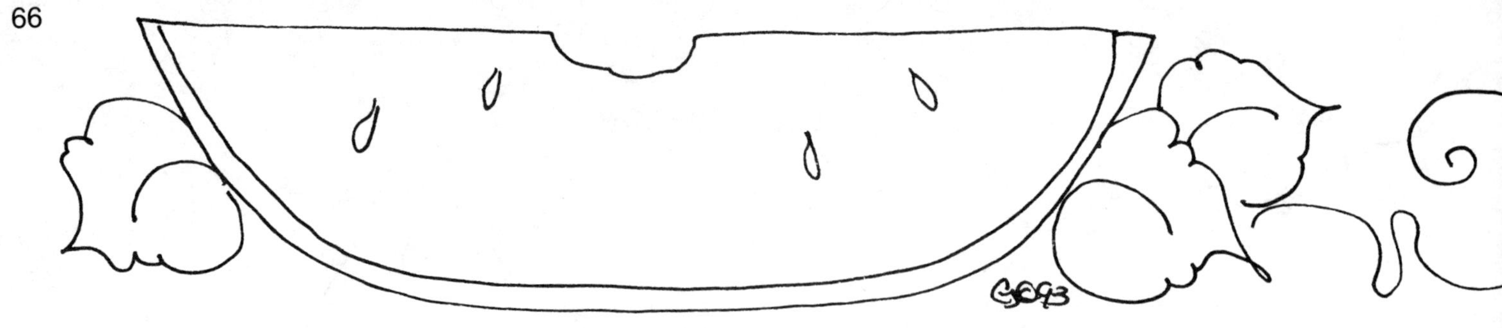

WATERMELON

PALETTE-Deco Art Americana

Black Forest Green
Burnt Umber
Buttermilk
Calico Red
Coral Rose
Country Red
Dusty Rose
Plantation Pine
Moon Yellow
Forest Green

Miscellaneous

Liquitex Modeling Paste
Dried Flowers: Larkspur

Build up the edges of the leaf with modeling paste. A round brush seemed to work well for this.

1. Wash the entire board and the small pieces of watermelon with Buttermilk plus touch of Dusty Mauve.
2. The red sections of all the pieces of watermelon are sponged wet in wet. First sponge Dusty Rose, then Coral Rose and last Country Red.
3. Float with Buttermilk next to the rind.
4. Wash all of the green areas with Plantation Pine. Float all of the shadows first with Forest Green. Then float the darker ones with Black Forest Green plus a touch of Burnt Umber. Float the highlights with Moon Yellow.
5. Wash a little Calico Red on the leaves and the watermelon.
6. Use the dark green mix for the lettering, tendrils, and the edges of the board.
7. Do the seed with a #4 filbert an thinned Burnt Umber paint. Float the shadows on the bottoms of the seeds with Burnt Umber and the highlight with Moon Yellow.
8. Spatter all of the pieces with the dark green mix.

TIGER CUB BOOK ENDS

PALETTE-Deco Art Americana

Black
Lemon Yellow
Cadmium Orange
Uniform Blue
Dioxazine Purple
French Blue Grey
Buttermilk
Terra Cotta
Dark Pine
Burnt Umber
Raw Sienna
Country Red
White

1. Base the tiger in Terra Cotta. Float all of the shadows with Burnt Umber. Stipple the highlights first with Raw Sienna plus a touch of Buttermilk and then with more Buttermilk. With a grainier streak all of the Black stripes.
2. Base the eyes in White. Float the iris in the eye with Dark Pine plus a touch of Lemon Yellow. Float around the edge of this with Dark Pine.
3. Base the book ends in Buttermilk
4. Base his shirt in White plus a touch of French Blue Grey.
5. With Country Red stripe his shirt, float the apple, stripe on the ball, and the cover of the book.
6. Float the shadows on his shirt and one stripe on the ball with Uniform Blue.
7. Float the leaf and one stripe on the ball in Dark Pine plus a touch of Burnt Umber.
8. Float the highlights on his shirt with White.
9. Stripe the rest of the ball in Dioxazine Purple, Cadmium Orange and Lemon Yellow.
10. Do his nose, the pupils and lashes, and the lettering on the book with Black.
11. Float his nose, lip, and inside of his ears with Buttermilk plus a touch of Country Red. Highlight all facial features with a dot of White.

B is for
Ball

TIGER CUB BOOK ENDS

YOU !

I LOVE TO READ

JACOB'S BABY BOOK

A B C

STRUTTIN'

PALETTE-Deco Art Americana

Dazzling Metallics:

Black Pearl	Teal Pearl	Green Pearl
Venetian Gold	Ice Blue	White Pearl
Shimmering Silver		

So Soft Fabric Dyes:

Dark Chocolate	Terra Cotta

Heavy Metal: Glimmering Silver

Acrylic: Gooseberry

Shimmering Pearls:

Christmas Green	Golden Yellow	Christmas Red
Ultra Blue		

Miscellaneous:

2 Craft eyes
11 Sapphire Rhinestone
10 Crystal Rhinestones

1. Base the body in Ice Blue. Float the shadows with a mix of Ultra Blue and Black Pearl. Highlight with White Pearl plus a touch of Ice Blue.
2. Base the wings in a mix of Shimmering Silver plus a touch of Black Pearl. Highlight with White Pearl.
3. With a grainier (new brush like comb or rake) and a mix of 1/2 Venetian Gold and 1/2 White Pearl draw the strands out from the vein of each feather . Add a little more White and do the highlights.
4. With a mix of Terra Cotta and White Pearl base in the beak and the legs and the bronze area at the ends of the feathers. Float the shadows on the legs and the beak in Dark Chocolate and the highlights with Golden Yellow.
5. With Teal Pearl base in the teal area at the end of the feather, the dark spot in the middle is Ultra Blue plus a touch of Black. With the grainier and a mix of 1/2 Green Pearl and 1/2 Christmas Green pull out the strands around the bronze area at the end of the feather. On top of the green pull out a little Golden Yellow. With Golden Yellow line around the bronze area.
6. Base the shoes and the lettering in Gooseberry. Wash the shoes and the cheeks with Christmas Red. Float the shadows on the red areas with Dark Chocolate. Base the sole of the shoes in Dark Chocolate plus White. Float the shadows with Black and the highlights with White.
7. Do all of the accent stars in White.
8. Accent the letters, stars, and here and there on the peacock with Glimmering Clear.

Glue the sapphire rhinestones at the end of each feather, the crystal ones in the stars and the eyes.

GOOD MORNING SUNSHNE

WATCHES: STAN BROWN'S

COLOR WHEEL ROSES

TIME FOR LOVE

WATCHES
COLOR WHEEL OF ROSES
TIME FOR LOVE
GOOD MORNING SUNSHINE

PALETTE-Deco Art Americana

Antique Gold
Black
Mocha
Calico Red
True Blue
Dioxazine Purple
Indian Turquoise
Burnt Umber
Plantation Pine
Dark Pine
Cadmium Orange
Black Forest Green
Moon Yellow
Cranberry Wine
White

All of the watches are done with thin washes. The directions with the watches say use thin paint or you may plug up the hands.

GOOD MORNING SUNSHINE

1. Wash the sky with True Blue.
2. Float each section on the rainbow with the paint on the bottom with Calico Red, Antique Gold, Dioxazine Purple, Dark Pine plus a little White and last with True Blue.
3. Wash the sunshine in Moon Yellow. Float the shadows with Antique Gold. Float the cheeks with Calico Red.
4. Wash the grass in Plantation Pine with this color float a little darker around the flowers.
5. Pat in the pink flowers with White plus a touch of Calico Red. Float the shadows on these with Calico Red. Pat in the blue flowers with Indian Turquoise plus White. Float the shadows on these with Indian Turquoise.
6. Line everything and do the facial features with Burnt Umber.

COLOR WHEEL OF ROSES

1. Pat a circle of one color for each rose, Calico Red, Antique Gold, True Blue, Dioxazine Purple, Dark Pine, Cadmium Orange. Float the bottom edge and the inside of the bowl with the same color.
2. Wash the center of the watch with True Blue. Wash around the roses and in towards the center with Black Forest Green.
3. Float all of the petals on the roses with White.
4. Do the leaves and the tendrils in Black Forest Green.
5. Do the accent dots with White.

TIME FOR LOVE

1. For the background wash the stripes first in True Blue and then line with Cranberry Wine.
2. Wash the bunny suit in Calico Red plus a touch of White. Float the shadows in with Cranberry Wine, float the highlights with White.
3. Wash the heart in True Blue, float the edges with the same.
4. Wash the face and hands with Mocha. Do the hair around her face with Burnt Umber. Float the cheeks lightly with Calico Red.
5. Line everything and do the lettering in Black.

TO PAINT

STRUTTIN' LIKE A PEA

OCK
ON SATURDAY NIGHT
BAGAVAILABLE:
STAN BROWN'S

Sunflower
Seeds
25¢

SUNNY WELCOME

SUNNY WELCOME

PALETTE-Deco Americana

Antique Gold
Jade Green
Burnt Umber
Moon Yellow
Toffee
Gooseberry
Black
Light Cinnamon
Deep Teal
French Blue Grey
Berry Red
Lemon Yellow
Crimson Tide
Plantation Pine
White

Miscellaneous

2 Yds. Paper Twist
2 Yds. Raffia
12 Hearts 1/2"
5 Hearts 1"
Liquitex Modeling Paste

The faces of the sunflowers are done first with modeling paste. This can be applied with a palette knife or by stippling but it is close to 1/2" thick.

The background of the board is done wet in wet. Coat first with White and then streak lightly with French Blue Grey.

1. Base all of the stems and the leaves in Jade Green plus a touch of Plantation Pine. Float the shadows on the stems and the leaves that make up the hands with Plantation Pine. Float the highlights on these areas with Jade Green and then Moon Yellow. Float the shadows on the leaves that make up the skirt with Deep Teal, when dry wash with a little Crimson Tide. Float the highlights on these leaves with Deep Teal plus a touch of White, when dry wash with Gooseberry.

2. Base the petals on the flowers with Antique Gold plus a touch of Moon Yellow. Float the shadows on the petals with Burnt Umber. Float the highlights with White plus a touch of Moon Yellow. Wash the petals to the top of the flower with a little Lemon Yellow.

3. Stipple the faces wet in wet. First stipple Toffee, then all around the edge working towards the center with Light Cinnamon, then a little clear to the outside edge with Burnt Umber.

4. Float the cheeks and base the dark hearts in a mix of Gooseberry plus a touch of Berry Red. Float the outside edge of these hearts with Crimson Tide. Base the light hearts in Gooseberry plus a touch of White and float the outside edge with Berry Red.

5. Base the eyes and line the facial features all in Black. Highlight with White.

6. Do the dots around the face, upper with Toffee and lower with Burnt Umber plus a touch of Black. Do all lettering with this mix.

BOOK LIST

Vol.	Title	No.	Price
Vol. 1	"His and Hers" by Susan Scheewe	101	$6.50
Vol. 5	"So Dear To My Heart" by Susan Scheewe	105	$5.50
Vol. 6	"Brushed With Elegance" by Susan Scheewe	106	$5.50
Vol. 7	"Paint'n Patch" by Susan Scheewe	107	$5.50
Vol. 11	"I Love To Paint" by Susan Scheewe	111	$6.50
Vol. 14	"Enjoy Painting Animals" by Susan Scheewe	114	$6.50
Vol. 17	"Countryside Reflections" by Susan Scheewe	161	$6.50
Vol. 18	"Mostly Landscapes" by Susan Scheewe	216	$7.50
Vol. 19	"Gift Of Painting" by Susan Scheewe	230	$7.50
Vol. 20	"Simply Country Watercolors" by Susan Scheewe	257	$7.50
Vol. 21	"Simply Watercolor" by Susan Scheewe T.V. Book	260	$11.95
Vol. 4	"Keepsake Sampler" by Camille and Susan Scheewe	200	$6.50
Vol. 1	"Painting It's Our Bag" by Bev Hink/Susan Scheewe	193	$7.50
Vol. 2	"Painting It's Our Bag" by Bev Hink/Susan Scheewe	209	$7.50
Vol. 1	"Loving You" by Susan and Camille Scheewe	224	$7.50
Vol. 1	"Western Images" by Backy Anothony	186	$6.50
Vol. 3	"Fantasy Flowers II" by Georgia Bartlett	129	$6.50
Vol. 5	"Soft Petals" by Georgia Bartlett	171	$6.50
Vol. 6	"Painting Fantasy Flowers" by Georgia Bartlett	215	$7.50
Vol. 1	"Painting A Barrel of Fun" by Donna Bell	194	$6.50
Vol. 2	"Painting A Barrel of Fun" by Donna Bell	201	$7.50
Vol. 3	"Barnscapes and More" by Donna Bell	218	$7.50
Vol. 4	"Countryscapes" by Donna Bell	249	$7.50
Vol. 5	"Painter to Painter" by Donna Bell	263	$7.50
Vol. 1	"Kids and Water" by Joyce Benner	234	$7.50
Vol. 1	"Natures Palette" by Carol Binford	248	$7.50
Vol. 1	"Oil Painting The Easy Way" by Bill Blackman	219	$7.50
Vol. 1	"Mini Mini More" by Terri and Nancy Brown	150	$6.50
Vol. 2	"Mini Mini More" by Terri and Nancy Brown	151	$6.50
Vol. 4	"Heritage Trails" by Terri and Nancy Brown	169	$6.50
Vol. 1	"Windows of My World" by Jackie Clafin	174	$6.50
Vol. 2	"Windows of My World" by Jackie Clafin	181	$7.50
Vol. 3	"I'm Partial To Flowers" by Ellie Cook	157	$6.50
Vol. 4	"Enjoy Watercolor" by Ellie Cook	210	$7.50
Vol. 5	"Watercolor Memories" by Ellie Cook	246	$7.50
Vol. 1	"Santa and Sams" by Bobi Dolara	258	$7.50
Vol. 2	"Vintage Peace" by Bobi Dolara	270	$7.50
Vol. 2	"Expressions In Oil" by Dolores Egger	164	$6.50
Vol. 4	"Expressions In Oil" by Dolores Egger	239	$7.50
Vol. 1	"Victorian Days" by Gloria Gaffney	240	$7.50
Vol. 2	"Days Of Heaven" by Gloria Gaffney	252	$7.50
Vol. 3	"Winter Song" by Gloria Gaffney	271	$7.50
Vol. 1	"Watercolor Made Easy" by Kathie George	190	$7.50
Vol. 2	"Watercolor Made Easy" by Kathy George	236	$7.50
Vol. 5	"The Sky's The Limit" by Jean Green	203	$6.50
Vol. 1	"The Way I Started" by Gary Hawk	120	$6.00
Vol. 1	"Roses Are For Everyone" by Bill Huffaker	!45	$7.50
Vol. 3	"Natures Beauty" by Bill Huffaker	177	$6.50
Vol. 1	"Holiday Gathering" by Angie Hupp	267	$7.50
Vol. 1	"Copper, Silver, Brass and Glass" by Susan Jenkins	211	$6.50
Vol. 3	"Anyone Can Watercolor" by Ken Johnston	119	$6.50
Vol. 1	"Happy Heart Happy Home" by Cathy Jones	241	$7.50
Vol. 1	"Watercolor Fun and Easy" by Beverly Kaiser	243	$7.50
Vol. 1	"Backroads of My Memory" by Geri Kisner	225	$7.50
Vol. 2	"Backroads of My Memory" by Geri Kisner	245	$7.50
Vol. 1	"Country's Edge" by Shirley Koenig	179	$7.50
Vol. 2	"Country's Edge" by Shirley Koenig	212	$6.50
Vol. 1	"Love Lives Here" by Mary Lynn Lewis	170	$6.50
Vol. 2	"Love Lives Here" by Mary Lynn Lewis	185	$6.50
Vol. 3	"Love Lives Here" by Mary Lynn Lewis	195	$6.50
Vol. 1	"Ducks and Geese" by Jean Lyles	172	$6.50
Vol. 1	"Huckleberry Horse" by Hanna Long	269	$7.50
Vol. 1	"Creative Quill" by Claudia Nice	133	$6.50
Vol. 2	"Barnyards and Billygoats" by Claudia Nice	134	$6.50
Vol. 3	"Wings and Wildflowers" by Claudia Nice	135	$6.50
Vol. 5	"Pen and Brush Animals" by Claudia Nice	137	$6.50
Vol. 6	"Journey of Memories" by Claudia Nice	166	$6.50
Vol. 7	"Scenes From Seasons Past" by Claudia Nice	183	$7.50
Vol. 8	"A Taste of Summer" by Claudia Nice	223	$7.50
Vol. 1	"Wildflower Sampler" by Bev Norman	191	$7.50
Vol. 1	"Stepping Stones" by Judy Nutter	121	$6.50
Vol. 1	"Whimsical Critters" by Lori Ohlson	228	$7.50
Vol. 1	"Holiday Medley" by Nina Owens	265	$7.50
Vol. 1	"Oh Those Little Rascals" by Diane Permenter	247	$7.50
Vol. 1	"Rustic Charms" by Sharon Rachal	175	$6.50
Vol. 2	"Rustic Charms" by Sharon Rachal	199	$7.50
Vol. 3	"Rustic Charms" by Sharon Rachal	217	$6.50
Vol. 4	"Rustic Charms" by Sharon Rachal	238	$7.50
Vol. 5	"Rustic Charms Florals" by Sharon Rachal	261	$7.50
Vol. 1	"Painting Flowers With Augie" by Augie Reis	152	$6.50
Vol. 1	"Forever In My Heart" by Diane Richards	188	$6.50
Vol. 2	"Memories In My Heart" by Diane Richards	189	$7.50
Vol. 3	"Forever In My Heart" by Diane Richards	205	$7.50
Vol. 5	"Memories In Your Heart" by Diane Richards	237	$7.50
Vol. 6	"Angels In My Stocking" by Diane Richards	254	$7.50
Vol. 7	"Nostalgic Dreams" by Diane Richards	273	$7.50
Vol. 1	"Realistic Florals and More" by Judy Sleight	233	$7.50
Vol. 2	"Painting Realism" by Judy Sleight	272	$7.50
Vol. 1	"Soft and Misty Paintings" by Kathy Snider	204	$7.50
Vol. 2	"Soft and Misty Paintings" BY Kathy Snider	229	$7.50
Vol. 3	"Soft and Misty Paintings" by Kathy Snider	251	$7.50
Vol. 1	"Creations In Canvas,...and More" by Carol Spooner	256	$7.50
Vol. 1	"Country Primitives" by Maxine Thomas	274	$7.50
Vol. 1	"Rise and Shine" by Jolene Thompson	214	$7.50
Vol. 2	"Garden Gate" by Jolene Thompson	250	$7.50
Vol. 1	"Count Your Blessings" by Chris Thornton	176	$7.50
Vol. 5	"Count Your Blessings" by Chris Thornton	213	$7.50
Vol. 6	"Share Your Blessings" by Chris Thornton	226	$7.50
Vol. 7	"Blessings" by Chris Thornton	255	$7.50
Vol. 8	"Christmas Blessings" by Chris Thornton	266	$7.50
Vol. 9	"Blessings For The Home" by Chris Thornton	275	$7.50
Vol. 4	"Friends We've Known" by Gene Waggoner	187	$6.50
Vol. 5	"Friends Are Forever" by Gene Waggoner	231	$7.50
Vol. 1	"Fantasy Folks" by Don Weed	123	$6.60
Vol. 2	"Painting The Clowns" by Don Weed	198	$7.50
Vol. 5	"Daydreams & Sweet Shirts II" by Don & Lynn Weed	208	$7.50
Vol. 1	"Floral Fabrics and Watercolors" by Sally Williams	262	$7.50
Vol. 1	"Friendship Garden" by Shirley Wingert	253	$7.50
Vol. 1	"Colored Pencil Made Easy" by Jane Wunder	232	$7.50
Vol. 2	"Colored Pencil Made Easy" by Jane Wunder	242	$7.50
Vol. 3	"The Beauty of Colored Pencil and Ink Drawing" by Jane Wunder	259	$7.50
Vol. 1	"Something Special For Everyone" by Mildred Yeiser	158	$6.50
Vol. 2	"Something Special For Everyone" by Mildred Yeiser	178	$6.50
Vol. 4	"Something Special For Everyone" by Mildred Yeiser	235	$7.50
Vol. 5	"Soft and Gentle Paintings" by Mildred Yeiser	268	$7.50

VIDEOS

"THE GIFT OF PAINTING, SIMPLY WATERCOLOR" VIDEO - By Susan Scheewe Brown. Guided instruction through tools and techniques for the beginning watercolorist.......................$24.95

"THE GIFT OF PAINTING" VIDEO - By Susan Scheewe Brown. Problems and solutions when painting oil landscapes. The video runs 90-minutes while two landscapes are completed....$24.95

*PLEASE ADD $3.00 for handling and postage, PER TAPE.
Sorry, but we must have a "NO REFUND-NO RETURN" policy.
Add $1.75 for First Book and shipping
Add $1.25 per each additional book.
U.S. CURRENCY
Prices Subject to change without notice

SHIPPING ____________
BOOK TOTAL ____________
TAPE TOTAL ____________
TOTAL ____________

NAME ____________
ADDRESS ____________
CITY/STATE/ZIP ____________
PHONE (   ) ____________

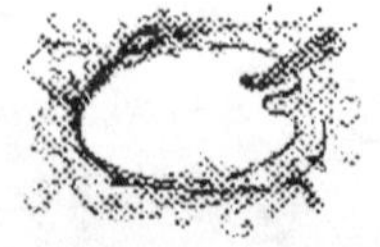

Susan Scheewe Publications
13435 N.E. Whitaker Way
Portland, Or. 97230
PH. (503) 254-9100 FAX (503) 252-9508

MASK
PAGE 56

PLANTER WAGON
PAGES 36, 37

WATERMELON
PAGES 64, 65, 66

ONION KEEPER AND
GARLIC KEEPER
PAGES 61, 62